Praise For *The Ministry of Business*

"In my business career, I have concluded there are two forms of education critical to professional success. The first comes from what you learn in school, and the second begins after you graduate. The life lessons learned through many years of experience are what molds a young professional into a seasoned and wise leader of people. *The Ministry of Business* condenses years' worth of experience into one concise read. I encourage anyone who wants to be a successful leader to accelerate your life years ahead by reading this incredible book."

- Rulon Stacey,
PhD, FACHE; CEO of Poudre Valley Health System; Author of *Over Our Heads*

"Success in business is governed by our individual definition of success. This book helps develop a wise definition, and then provides practical advice on how to achieve that success."

- J. Lawrence Richards,
President of LDS Business College

"I love a good story that motivates me to change and to improve, and *The Ministry Of Business* does just that! By providing the knowledge and motivation necessary to launch yourself into a future of leadership and service, this book offers a great step toward finding long-lasting happiness."

- Dr. Max L. Checketts,
Vice President of Academics at Brigham Young University—Hawaii

"The teachings in this book are simple, yet profound and universal. Your life will be blessed as you apply these principles to your personal and professional activities."

- Mark Tingey,

President's Council at Brigham Young University—Idaho

"I endorse the marvelous concepts found within *The Ministry of Business*. Having had experience both living and teaching these concepts, I can attest that they have already changed the lives of many, whether young or old, college student or budding entrepreneur. I will be forever grateful for the changes these concepts bring into the lives of all those who embrace them."

- Moses Armstrong,

Owner of Essential Foods, New Zealand; Director of Launching Leaders in Auckland, New Zealand

---

"*The Ministry of Business* outlines a powerful formula for success in business and in life. Steve Hitz reveals the secret: never separate the two. Live by the same correct principles in your business and personal life, and you will experience great success!"

- Michael Leonard,

Executive Professor of Marketing at Monfort College of Business, University of Northern Colorado

---

"The principles so well expressed in this book are always true, regardless of the country, market, or hemisphere in which you live and work. I unreservedly recommend this book to anyone who wants increased happiness, contentment, and success."

- Richard Ball,
Managing Director of Anytime Fitness New Zealand, Ltd.; Managing Director of Yafa Plus, Ltd.

"To the degree they are applied to your life, the powerful principles outlined in this book can have a dramatic impact on your personal development and business success. The easy-to-understand approach of *The Ministry of Business* provides a road map for a lifetime of development."

- Craig Nelson,
Vice President of Advancement at LDS Business College

"The powerful spiritual principles which are shared in this book will bless the lives of all those who apply them. For small business owners, entrepreneurs, CEOs, and industry leaders, this book is truly a must read! In a clear manner, *The Ministry of Business* integrates spiritual and business principles which can guide one to achieve success in every aspect of one's life."

- Elia Gourgouris,
PhD; President of LDS Coaching

"I found this book to be an exhilarating read. Steve and James have passed on powerful principles for life that they have learned from both mentors and the experiences of living. I was so impressed that I have begun to apply these principles to my own life, with careful attention as to how I might be an effective mentor to others. I highly recommend this book as a powerful tool to achieve a clear, values-based life plan that impressively integrates healthy personal desires with spiritual direction, all while recruiting and utilizing wise mentorship. It's about the synergy of principled interconnectedness, and it's a total package for success."

- Wallace Dudley,

PsyD; Clinical Psychologist

"*The Ministry of Business* could not be closer to the truth when it comes to helping those who wish to be successful. My only regret is that I did not discover these simple steps when I was younger. I wholeheartedly endorse this book to all those who wish to 'make their mark' in this life."

- Jay Seymour,

LDS Area Employment Manager of the Pacific Area

the ministry of business
how correct principles magnify business success

Steven A. Hitz with James W. Ritchie
Foreword by Hyrum W. Smith

ISBN-13: 978-1475038026
ISBN-10: 147503802X

Book design and illustrations by Fly Creative, Ltd. New Zealand
Editing by Charles Limley

First Edition

Printed in the United States of America

To our beloved children, who are our best friends and mentors: in you we find the joy of living.

- Steve and Ginger Hitz

To the four groups of people for whom I pray daily: my children, my grandchildren, my missionaries, and my students. May you achieve your righteous desires, and do it with nobility.

- James Ritchie

Table of Contents

Foreword

When I began working closely with Steve Hitz, I was most struck by his outward contentment. He consistently wore a smile of acceptance and love rather than an expression of judgment. He seemed at peace with himself and with others, never hinting at distress or fear.

So it came as a surprise when I found out he was a successful entrepreneur—I had become too accustomed to the image of the highly stressed business owner, the exact antithesis of the man I was then getting to know. It was both relieving and intriguing to meet someone like Steve.

As I became more familiar with Steve and his wife, Ginger, they shared with me their story of entrepreneurial and financial success. They explained to me that the key to their achievements had been learning just how interconnected their spiritual and temporal lives really are. Living correct spiritual principles had become a life foundation upon which they were able to build both a happy family and a multi-million dollar business.

Steve continued on, explaining to me just how much he'd grown to value the role and work of mentors. In fact, he credited much of his success to lessons he'd learned from James Ritchie, one of his most influential life mentors. And it was at this point that we began making some very interesting connections.

As it turns out, James is also a close friend and associate of mine. At the time that my company, Franklin Quest, was merging with Covey Leadership to become Franklin Covey, I convinced James to come out of retirement (which he accomplished at age 35) to become the company's national sales manager. James did an incredible job, and he played a critical role in helping Franklin Covey grow into a billion dollar corporation.

Through our work together, I had become familiar with James and his personal business philosophies, many of which aligned very closely with the type of values-oriented business strategies I'd spent my own career developing, teaching, and writing about.

Given both my prior experience with James and my growing relationship with Steve, I was curious to learn more about the ways these two had interacted. The opportunity to see these two men together in action came when I was invited to speak at the Great Ideas Conference, hosted by Brigham Young University—Hawaii. At the time, James and his wife were serving as directors of the university's Willes Center for International Entrepreneurship.

During this conference, I learned that James and Steve—along with several other powerful and dynamic leaders—had organized a team of successful entrepreneurs and businesspeople to teach young adults the power of coupling their spiritual lives with their temporal lives. This team had put together a compelling curriculum and was in the process of preparing a program called Launching Leaders that would carry this curriculum to young people around the world.

I was fascinated by this project, and monitored its progress as it began to unfold, beginning with its pilot program in New Zealand. At the close of Launching Leaders' first intake of students, my wife and I were invited to attend the graduation ceremony and to teach a seminar on "Belief Windows," a powerful concept I had recently developed and had been teaching internationally.

I was taken aback by the powerful impact Launching Leaders had in the lives of its students. The young adults, mentors, and leaders who had participated in it had embraced the program's teachings, and doing so had changed their lives for the better. Launching Leaders not only taught professional and financial success, it enabled individuals to recognize and attain their Divine Potential. This was truly amazing stuff.

It was during this trip to New Zealand that Steve told me he'd decided to write a book. "Do tell," I responded. He explained to me that he wanted to title the book *The Ministry of Business*, and in it, he wanted to outline the principles he felt most helpful in attaining the type of entrepreneurial and financial success he and Ginger had achieved. The overarching claim of this book would be that through living correct moral and spiritual principles, anybody can attain personal, professional, and financial success, independence, and happiness.

When I told him I liked the title and the idea, he went for the kill: "Would you write the foreword?" In Jewish terms this is called "chutzpah," and it worked. Right there, on the spot, I said, "I'd love to."

Nearly a year after this conversation, Steve presented me with the manuscript. As I read his and Ginger's stories, and became familiar with the ways in which the principles expounded throughout the text have changed their lives and continue to change lives around the world, I was glad I'd made the commitment to write the foreword.

I now write these words and offer my support of the concepts taught in this book as a true believer—as someone who has lived according to them and who has witnessed time and again the impact these principles make in the lives of any willing to adopt them.

In many ways, *The Ministry of Business* is a story about a mentor (James Ritchie) and his students (Steve and Ginger Hitz). This story highlights both the ways their own lives have become successful, as well as the ways they and their associates are now working to change the world by adhering to and teaching the principles outlined in what you're about to read.

Steve has done a masterful job of weaving the lessons learned through 30 years of experience into a concise and meaningful treatise on success and business. This book is not a new spin on old ideas. I've read many of the established "classics" of business literature, and while many of them are referred to in this book, the principles taught in *The Ministry of Business* are different. They are powerful. They are complete. They are real.

I have never read—nor will you read—a more powerful assertion than this: The marriage of great spiritual principles with great business principles will enable you to achieve your greatest and noblest dreams. This is the foundational belief of *The Ministry of Business*.

Steve wholeheartedly understands that his entrepreneurial success is part of a greater purpose. For him, business is not an end in itself; business is simply one piece in the much larger objective of realizing his Divine Potential through serving others and giving back to this world.

Ultimately, this book highlights and explains the eternal worth inherent in each and every human being, and that includes you. It serves as a practical guide for allowing this knowledge to lend greater purpose, and in the end greater success, to your career. Steve practices what he preaches, and his entrepreneurial and financial success stands as a testament to the power of what this book teaches.

As Steve continually maintains, there are no coincidences in life, and the intersections of my life path with the life paths of the Ritchies and the Hitzes are nothing short of miraculous. To my friends of all faiths, I extend an invitation with a promise: Read this book and live by its teachings, and your life will change for the better, forever.

- Hyrum W. Smith, 2012

Co-Founder and Former CEO of FranklinCovey

Chairman and CEO of Legacy Quest, Inc.

Author and Lecturer

Acknowledgements

We are first and foremost indebted to those inspired leaders, teachers, and friends who have gone before and developed works of relevance and insight—wells from which we've filled our buckets.

The principles outlined in *The Ministry of Business* have been crystalized with the help of Charles Limley, the masterful editor of this project.

Noting the danger of inadvertently leaving out some who have greatly shaped our lives, we feel to thank our beloved parents, our amazing children, mentors such as Clyde and Rita Harris, James and Carolyn Ritchie, Glonda Garrett, and so many more. We would not have survived the journey without believing and encouraging friends such as the Porters, Bowens, and the Kross and Ames families. Thanks also to Layne Dearden, creative writing professor extraordinaire, for inspiring the confidence to write.

We have been greatly influenced for good by our spiritual leaders, such as Grant Brimhall, Russell McClure, Lynn Morgan, Bill True, Keith Allred, Mike Palmer, and others whose smiles and confidence have consistently provided the impetus to move forward even in the face of difficulties.

Also, we thank and acknowledge our administrative assistants, Kimberly Fischer and Kerstin Alvarez, whose ongoing contributions make possible so many things.

Finally, for all the brave Kiwis who were willing to take a chance on Launching Leaders, and to Terry and Mary Pitts, for making it happen: Kia Ora.

Introduction

"Happiness is the meaning and the purpose of life, the whole aim and end of human existence."

- Aristotle

Experiential Credibility

More important than chronicling the business successes Ginger and I have enjoyed, this book works to outline the principles and techniques from which these successes arise. In reality, these concepts are not ours alone, but are products of the ideas, experiences, and efforts of a whole host of teachers, associates, friends, partners, and mentors.

Recognizing the truly collaborative nature of these teachings, this book contains contributions from various individuals; these contributions are powerful supplements to my words. Thus, while I remain the primary speaker throughout the text, there will be sections in which someone else speaks, sharing his or her own perspectives and stories. The speakers of these sections will be noted in the section heading, and if no name is given, then the words of that section are mine. Paying attention to each section heading will therefore allow you to clearly follow who's speaking and will greatly enhance your reading experience.

The Ministry of Business is intended for all people of faith, and will provide a foundation of spiritual and business principles from which to build a life of greatness. Whether your aim is to enhance your professional career, learn to plan and set life goals effectively, or become a successful entrepreneur, the principles you're about to read will be of relevance to you and your life.

Ginger and I are not graduates of formal academia; we are students of life. This is not to say, however, that we downplay the role of academic education. In fact, we wholeheartedly support and strongly encourage formal education, of which all our children are participants, and to which our family has donated much to the establishment of scholarships.

Fully recognizing the importance of education—especially the need to continue learning well beyond the classroom—the writings of this book are born largely from the experiences we have lived firsthand. We have lived both the entrepreneur's dreams and nightmares, and having survived to tell about it, believe that our experiences in the real world of effectively building businesses offer at least a modicum of credibility to our words.

A very small percentage of business owners are actually successful in building an enterprise and successfully crossing the finish line. We have been fortunate enough to do so, and we continue to build and operate a variety of profitable business ventures. For example, we— and it is important to note here that "we" includes a broad network of devoted partners and colleagues—built a business from scratch that currently has well over 1,000 associates and delivers services in all 50 of the United States. We also run our own investment company with significant holdings in real estate, farming, and banking.

In some ways, we see ourselves as not unlike well known individuals such as Steve Jobs and Bill Gates, who found success only after living through challenges, failures, and mistakes. We, too, have trudged through our own sets of difficulties and trials before finally coming out on top. This journey has certainly brought the financial well being, self-reliance, and security we were working for, but beyond that, it taught us lessons far greater and more meaningful than any amount of net financial worth.

Our business successes have also led to several opportunities to work in teaching, training, and mentorship positions. In our associations with universities, we have reviewed and judged hundreds of business plans, become mentors to many students and aspiring entrepreneurs, and watched as the principles we've shared with them were implemented into their plans and strategies with significant success.

Throughout all of this work—whether pursuing our own ventures or advising others in the pursuit of theirs—we have established a unique business culture that has stood the test of time and which has allowed for the personal growth of everyone we associate with. It is this culture that we now hope to share with you.

The Bigger Picture

The ideas we're about to discuss are adaptations of correct principles we've learned from the incredible mentors, businesspeople, authors, and associates around us. To them we owe a great debt of gratitude.

Above all else, though, we have learned and benefited from our friendship with Deity. Such a relationship carries with it a special and particularly powerful sense of spirituality, and if you understand that the God of Heaven looks upon His children without prejudice, loving them all equally, then you already have a sense of the hope and purpose we're talking about.

In discussing the importance of spirituality in our lives, we draw heavily from our beliefs as members of the Church of Jesus Christ of Latter-Day Saints. Consequently, we will refer to the centrality of having the Spirit of the Lord in our lives, especially in business. Because these are principles of truth, however, they may be applied to anybody's life, regardless of religion, belief system, or the words we use to describe them.

We have a deep and abiding love for most all religions, and believe the principles we adhere to are universal and eternal, relevant to your life and to everybody else's. Where we talk about the "Spirit of the Lord," then, you may talk about your "inner voice," and we will all reach the same conclusions. The beauty of these spiritual principles is that when they're applied to your life, they become unique and customized to your particular lifestyle, goals, and needs. Take what we offer and build upon it by adding your own truths and goals.

Ultimately, what makes *The Ministry of Business* unique is that we have combined true and effective principles from the concrete and tangible business world with the truths taught in scripture to provide a framework or foundation that will be of great benefit to you in both your business and personal lives as you learn to apply them.

Those who know us also know that we don't believe any success we've experienced is ours alone, nor do we believe these successes would be possible without the grace of God. This book is therefore written with a fundamental belief that one's spiritual activity intersects with and impacts one's business activity. Real business success must be accompanied by spiritual success and the personal growth this facilitates.

True fulfillment in life is found in two ways: recognizing our divine natures and fulfilling the purpose of our being. First, we must understand that because we are human beings living on this earth, we have inherent worth as children of God. We are intimately connected to Deity. This knowledge will then help us realize that we have unlimited potential and great reasons for living. We are not intended to sit on the beach and watch the sun set every evening— as wonderful as this is, there is more to life. There is a purpose in our living, and the sooner we realize this, the better off we and the rest of humanity will be.

As you read, we hope you will feel excited and enthusiastic about the ideas you encounter—not because of the way they've affected us, but because of the ways they can fit into and impact your own life. Let the impressions and thoughts you have while reading plant themselves in your heart and mind. As they are nourished, a forest of friends, mentors, and events will spring into your life to help you build your own pathway to success.

The Lord, the Universe—whichever name you choose to call It—will come to your aid because no one succeeds alone—no one.

The Purpose

Owning a business of our own had never occurred to either Ginger or me. I grew up in a small town in northern Wyoming where my father, the hardest worker I've ever known, worked at the same company for 50 years. After returning from World War II, it was the only company he ever worked for. Growing up, my dream was to follow what I had seen my father do and earn a decent living working for somebody else.

Ginger grew up in southern California, where her father was a very successful fireman. While he did have some entrepreneurial aspirations, all attempts at achieving these desires fell short, so that for Ginger, the very thought of starting our own business conjured up feelings of worry and concern.

In February 1976, I left Wyoming for Los Angeles, where I served a two-year service and ministerial mission. This was a profound experience, and it changed many of my perspectives regarding my personal potential. Coming from a small town in Wyoming, where the only part of life we could call diverse was the area's interesting variety of wildlife, Los Angeles was an entirely new experience. Here, I was able to meet and become involved in the lives of people from all socioeconomic, racial, national, and linguistic backgrounds. In the Los Angeles area, the world had converged to seek a better life, and the diversity of it all was amazing and beautiful.

Through this experience, I quickly learned that God cares about all

His children, and that He speaks to us all with the same divine voice of love and peace. As I learned to value each new and colorful thread in the tapestry of humanity, my heart yearned to make a positive difference in as many lives as I could.

I also realized in a very personal way that God is intimately involved in the full spectrum of life, and that this spectrum extends well beyond my own little world. Consequently, my vision of who I was, who I could become, and what my place in this world could become expanded greatly.

While this was truly a powerful and eye-opening experience, these new perspectives also seemed to conflict with my old, somewhat limited expectations. I became confused about what to do with myself at the end of my missionary service.

Toward the end of these two years, I began to think seriously about what my career might be, and actually started drawing pictures of office doors, all marked with my name, "Steven A. Hitz," and a job title, "Attorney at Law," "Janitor," "Teacher." Visualizing myself in these different occupations, I spent a great deal of time praying to understand what it was the Lord would have me do. Although I never received any clear indication at that time as to a possible career path, I felt assured that if I lived according to my personal standards, everything would somehow work out.

A short time after completing my missionary service, in June 1978, Ginger and I were married. I felt—and continue to feel—extremely blessed, having found a partner whose faith in me is constant, regardless of my career decisions and changes. Her faith in me through the years of our marriage has allowed us to experience many things we may not have otherwise experienced, and I certainly feel that I "married up." I owe my grandest experiences of life largely to her.

When we were first married, we moved to Lovell, Wyoming, a small town just seven miles from where I grew up. Without any idea of what to do, I took several jobs: working the night shift loading train cars at a sugar factory, sweeping floors at a bentonite plant, and blowing insulation for a construction company.

Ginger, meanwhile, worked at a furniture store that doubled as a funeral home (that's right—a funeral home! Feel free to recline in a La-Z-Boy, but don't doze off for too long!), and soon took a second job in the offices of the sugar factory at which I worked. I finished work at 8 a.m., the same time Ginger began work, and we'd pass each other every morning outside the factory.

These were interesting times. We rented a small apartment in a retirement home complex, and would sometimes come home to see neighbors being packed away in body bags, taken to the same funeral home where Ginger worked.

We felt good about working hard to support each other, and whether it was sweeping floors for eight hours straight, blowing insulation into roofs, loading sugar beets into train cars, keeping books, or managing a funeral home office, we were grateful for our jobs. It soon became clear, however, that we were not making enough to meet our expenses—we couldn't even fill up the car with enough gas to drive the seven miles to my parents' house so they could feed us!

The winter of 1978-1979 proved to be one of the coldest on record, dropping to as low as 40 below zero. During one of these cold, wet, and snowy afternoons, Ginger drove to the bentonite plant to pick me up after work. As I sludged through the thick and sticky mud, Ginger jumped out of the car and ran toward me. She excitedly told me she was pregnant with our first child. At that moment, the excitement in my mind quickly led to the question, "How will I take care of my family?" I knew the status quo wouldn't work. Doing what

I was then doing would not fulfill my wife's dreams, let alone my own. Something had to change.

Soon after Ginger became pregnant, the feeling that we needed to leave Wyoming overwhelmed her. At the time, the closest medical center was an hour and a half away, and Ginger just seemed to sense that this would become a problem for her and the new baby. Acting on these strong feelings, we packed everything we owned into a camper trailer and moved to California, where we could be closer to her family as well as larger hospitals.

Already struggling financially, leaving whatever jobs we currently held felt like a huge risk. But, because we recognized Ginger's strong feelings and impressions as personal inspiration from our loving Heavenly Father, we felt safe in making the move. We soon found work and quickly settled into our new life.

Our first child was born two months premature at the UCLA Medical Center, where he lived the first month of his life in an incubator. Had we not been in California at the time of his birth, so close to the skilled professionals and advanced equipment of UCLA, he would not have survived. Recognizing and following Ginger's personal inspiration thus became a key in saving the life of our new son.

As our time in California continued, it became even more clear how important this phase of our life was—we were meant to be exactly where we were. We eventually met and became connected with incredible mentors. The people, places, and events that comprised our life in California combined to create the scenarios in which we discovered new and amazing directions for our lives, and in which we began defining and working toward achieving our entrepreneurial dreams. In short, we discovered the people, ideas, skills, and passion needed to achieve our goals. We struck our personal "oil," and it all happened because we acted with faith on a spiritual prompting to leave our home in Wyoming.[1]

We believe in a verse of scripture that teaches us all good things will work together for the benefit of those who walk uprightly.[2] The experiences of our early life together certainly proved this to be true. Nothing about these experiences was coincidental, and they began to shape the pathway down which Providence would continue to lead us.

Looking back now, after 25 years of successfully starting and operating our own businesses, I have often pondered the pathway we have traveled. I understand now that this journey is truly compelling because the path we were to walk through all those years was lit before our feet no more than a few steps at a time. Only after exercising the faith to take those few visible steps were new sections of the path, and new actions in our life, revealed to us. This process is the way faith is developed, and if you have not yet connected the dots between faith and business risk, you will soon do so.

This book is a guide for anyone who believes, as we do, that there's more to life than just living a grand adventure and then dying. Life is certainly adventurous, exciting, and unpredictable, but it's also eternally meaningful. We were all born for a purpose.

One of the most important things I've learned from my personal experiences is that nothing about this life is coincidental—there are no coincidences. Things happen as part of a larger plan, and if we understand this, we will begin to glimpse the divine nature of our being. Many of the things some would call coincidental are, in reality, nothing short of miraculous.

This book is aimed at enhancing your entrepreneurial, career, and other life pursuits, although perhaps not in the traditional way. We will marry tested and proven business techniques and advice with spiritual truths and personal anecdotes. Because of the spiritual nature of this material, it will be important for you to listen carefully to the soft and quiet inner voice of your heart as you read. Recognize this inner voice as inspiration from God; this is the way God speaks to His children.

As you read, take time to ponder, meditate, or pray. The principles shared in this book are ones that have been customized by God to meet the specific obstacles and needs Ginger and I have faced, and they will similarly be adapted to fit your unique and individual life as well.

Finally, the question for you is why you would want to read this book? Simply put, the more you understand and incorporate into your life the principles of truth it shares, the happier your life will become. The knowledge that you have a divine purpose and potential, and that even now God is molding you and directing your life's pathway toward greatness, will enable you to bring greater happiness to the lives of those around you. And when you're making those around you happier, you yourself will experience a deep-seated contentment and joy unattainable in any other way.

The ultimate purpose of this book, then, is to provide you, the reader, hope and happiness. The principles it outlines will serve as a bridge, carrying you across the chasm of failure and unhappiness toward the Promised Land of personal success and happiness. When we realize there are important things for all of us to accomplish in this life, and as we begin to understand the divine purposes behind them, we will come to know of our divine heritage and destiny. Hope then springs eternal, knowing we are not alone, and that all things are possible for those who believe.

Bridge To Success

Life, Career & Entrepreneurial Success

MENTORS | FORMULA | PERSONAL CONSTITUTION | POWER OF COVENANTS | LIFE PLAN | GIVING BACK

PROMISED LAND

THE HARD WAY

Worldly Path

Chapter 01

Divine Guidance In Business

"Don't let the noise of others' opinions drown out your inner voice. And most important, have the courage to follow your heart and intuition. . . . Everything else is secondary."

- Steve Jobs[3]

Chapter 1 image - A lighthouse guides the path of ships through treacherous waters, as God lights our way before us.

As mentioned in the Introduction, one of the fundamental premises of this entire book is that your life is watched over by an all-powerful and all-loving God who has a plan for you and for every other individual. Periodically, small pieces of this plan will be revealed to you through personal spiritual promptings that urge you to make a particular decision, talk to a specific person, or to take some other action in your life. Trying to understand and follow these promptings is usually spoken of as "following your heart," and it's important to understand that what your heart "speaks" to you is in fact divine inspiration given to help guide your life down the unique pathways laid out by God.

This concept is crucial because it provides the fundamental understanding that as long as you follow your heart, giving heed to those moments of personal inspiration, and live according to your personal moral code, you will be blessed with even greater guidance and eventually with success. This doesn't mean that following your heart will necessarily make life easier, or that your success will be instantaneous, but it does provide a sense of confidence and security that will be of great benefit as you set out to achieve your goals.

Too Coincidental To Be Coincidental

In 1980, I was visiting with Mike Brookman, a friend and member of our local church congregation. Through the course of our conversation, he asked me how happy I was with my current job as sales representative and territory manager for a major home appliance outlet. I told him that while I loved this job in terms of income and schedule flexibility, I was feeling somewhat limited in terms of my ability to give back and contribute to society.

Mike then told me about his job. He was an insurance inspector, and was responsible for visiting insured businesses to assist them in their safety concerns and loss control efforts. Hearing him describe the way he was able to meet new people, travel to new places, and have new and unique experiences every day sounded intriguing.

I was so intrigued, in fact, that I tagged along with him one day and watched him work. I quickly saw that not only did this job offer unique experiences, but it was also something that made a difference for good. Mike's work was focused on helping business owners in their efforts to succeed.

Within a week, I interviewed with Mike's company and was hired on the spot. As I started this new occupation, Ginger and I were grateful that we were introduced to Mike, that our paths crossed at the exact time they did, and that he told me about this new and exciting career with which I could now make a positive mark on the world. If you're keeping track of coincidences—and you should be—meeting Mike at this precise moment in life is a big one.

By 1985, I had become the company's youngest regional manager, having been placed in charge of the entire southern California region, and had been named manager of the year three years in a row. My region was the company's largest and by far its most profitable. Life was good. Ginger and I had purchased our first home, were driving a new car, we were earning more in a quarter than I thought possible in a year, and our little family was growing.

Despite all this, Ginger and I were surprised when we both began having thoughts and feelings that perhaps this job wasn't an end in itself, but could in fact be preparing us for something even bigger. We began feeling desires to really stretch ourselves and start a company of our own. We were already happy and doing well, though, so why would these new feelings of entrepreneurialism be tempting us?

Neither Ginger nor myself had any idea why these feelings and ideas—these spiritual promptings—were occurring, but recognizing the importance of following the directions spoken by our hearts, we started Newsletter Marketing, a small company that developed newsletters for other businesses.

In those days, this was actually a relatively new idea. Al Gore had not yet invented the Internet, and email was nothing more than a vague, futuristic idea. Cell phones were rare, and if you had one, it looked like a telephone booth mounted in your car. In our spare time, we bought the newest Apple computer available and a laser printer, and went to work developing our first business. I hired my neighbor to sell local businesses on the idea, and we soon began signing many clients. In developing these newsletters, I became highly proficient in the software of the day, and while not a financial powerhouse in itself, this first entrepreneurial effort provided the exact tools I would need later on in life. As you will shortly see, Newsletter Marketing and the skills and knowledge it provided Ginger and I, was yet another coincidence in our life.

Around this same time, I received a phone call from my boss in Kansas City, asking me to come to the corporate home office for an interview. He wouldn't tell me what this meeting was about, and in light of my recent successes as a regional manager, I was feeling just a little puffed up as Ginger and I flew to Kansas City, daydreaming about offers to become National Loss Control Manager or to work in some other hotshot corporate position.

The real reason for this interview, however, would become a sign that our career path of insurance inspecting and auditing, and our newly inspired path of entrepreneurialism were beginning to converge.

Heading into the interview, I knew this company was not unlike others of its size—it certainly had its fair share of internal politics and hidden agendas. Fortunately, working so far away from corporate headquarters, and achieving such great success in southern California, I had been able to dodge most of this politicking.

Once I arrived in Kansas City, however, the politics finally caught up with me. I was surprised when I was called into the office of the company owner's wife, and not the office of the owner himself. She informed me that I had taken too much liberty by installing a $35 per month water cooler for my staff without her permission. This was the entire interview, the sole reason for flying all the way to Kansas City!

As I left this strange meeting and visited with other staff members, they were all apologetic for the political showdown. In a daze of confusion, Ginger and I flew back to Los Angeles. Despite our puzzlement, the flight home was filled with inspiration. It was becoming clear that perhaps our time with this company was drawing to its close, and we began formulating earnest plans to start a competing business, should this end up becoming our inspired path.

Ginger and I now had a concrete idea of a possible next step in life, but were still unsure. We knew we needed some truly inspired direction in our lives, and we turned to God for help and for answers to our questions.

As members of the LDS church, Ginger and I strongly believe in the ability of each individual to receive divine inspiration and guidance in his or her life. In The Book of Mormon, we read the story of a family fleeing persecution, and with direction from God, traveling toward a promised land. In a miracle not unlike God's provision of manna for the children of Israel as recorded in the Old Testament, the family in The Book of Mormon was given an instrument—something like a compass—through which God would communicate and provide directions. This instrument is called the Liahona, and since its appearance in the scriptural story, this object has become a metaphor for seeking and following God's guidance in our lives.

The type of guidance provided by the Liahona was just what Ginger and I needed as we tried to figure out whether or not we should stay in the increasingly uncomfortable position of my current occupation.

Also in the LDS church, we have special buildings called temples, where we believe we can find particularly strong connections to God and His spirit. These buildings are sacred to us, and we believe they provide a haven of reverence and peaceful quiet especially conducive to receiving and listening to spiritual promptings. In this way, visiting the temple is very similar to the narrated account of the Liahona. Thus it was that Ginger and I went to the closest temple and prayed for inspiration and direction. As we did so, we were both overcome with emotion as we felt our hearts confirm the need to leave our current company and put ourselves in a position to start our own.

Later that same year, there was talk that the company I worked for may be sold to a much larger corporation. I felt I would lose my identity and purpose in the setting of this new, larger company, and knew that if the buyout went through, it was the right time for my family and I to move on. When my company's president learned of my intentions, he immediately flew to Los Angeles and pleaded with Ginger and I to stay on board a while longer. Apparently our decision was adversely affecting the final buyout preparations. We told him we had already prayed about our decision, and months later, when the buyout was finally completed, we left.

Before leaving, however, Ginger and I had done our homework. Because I had an employment contract, we paid big bucks to have it thoroughly examined. We were assured that after the buyout, if I had never worked for the new entity (which I didn't since we left just as the buyout was finalized), then they would have no basis for a claim against me if I started my own competing company.

The stage was now fully set: we had successful insurance inspecting and auditing experience, we had acquired entrepreneurial and technological skills from Newsletter Marketing, we had legal advice and preparation, and we had the perfect opportunity to step out on our own. In 1988, I left the company and together, Ginger and I launched Golden Coast, an insurance auditing and loss control reporting company. It grew quickly and magnificently. Our customers were happy, our field representatives were happy, and Ginger and I were both happy and optimistic about the future.

In retrospect, the pathway leading us to the creation of Golden Coast is a network of seemingly coincidental events. What if we weren't in the right place at the right time to meet Mike? What if Mike hadn't asked me about my job and told me about his? What if I hadn't acted on my initial interest and applied for my first insurance inspecting job? What if Ginger and I hadn't simultaneously received the same puzzling desires to start our own businesses, and the spiritual confirmations to pursue these desires? What if my former employer had not sold his company when he did? If any one of these events had not occurred precisely when and how they did, Ginger and I may have never founded Golden Coast.

When viewed together and in relation to one another, these coincidences coalesce into a clear picture of divine guidance. We ourselves could certainly never have planned all these events, and there were just too many of them, all working together, to be blind chance. Our experiences taught us there is no such thing as coincidences, and that as long as we're willing to act with faith on the impressions and the inspirations of our hearts, God will clear a pathway—regardless of how confusing or unclear it may at times look to us—with which these impressions may be realized.

Making Lemonade

About eight months after opening Golden Coast, right around Christmas Eve, I was served with a lawsuit from my former employer. Despite the fact that there was no solid basis for them doing so (as our lawyer had accurately assured us), my old company was nonetheless attempting to sue me for leaving and starting a competing business.

In starting Golden Coast, we knowingly did nothing illegal, so our attorneys confidently took the lawsuit, understanding how shaky the basis for the lawsuit was. Still, the lawsuit would have to be fought, and for a brand new business (that first year of operation, we took only $4,000 as income in order to leave as much money as possible in the company), this unforeseen challenge would dangerously tap our already limited resources. Thankfully, we had followed the advice of a trusted mentor, and had saved enough money to be able to survive a full year with zero income.

As the lawsuit dragged on, I began to wonder whether that inner voice we had listened to and which had led us to start Golden Coast, wasn't in fact an imposter. I remember one day, I felt such despair that I sat alone in a dark closet, pouring my heart out to God in prayer. Did He really care about me and my family? If so, why would He allow this painful setback to continue dragging me down? Hadn't the inspiration to start this business originally come from Him anyway?

During these trying times of doubt, I learned more than ever to trust my wife and partner. Ginger maintained her faith that somehow these trials would work out in the end. While I felt weak, Ginger continued to believe that together we had limitless potential. Through consistent encouragement, wholehearted support, and sincere, heartfelt prayer, she helped me regain the vision of what we were trying to accomplish. And so it was, that with her determination as our anchor, we set out to turn lemons into lemonade.

During the time the lawsuit was active, I was temporarily enjoined against doing business in southern California. While this initially felt like a devastating blow, it actually catalyzed an incredible period of growth for Golden Coast.

Our original plan was to gradually expand, with the goal of covering all of California within five years. The lawsuit and its associated restrictions, however, forced us to seek out new regions for us to work in, and within a year, Golden Coast had opened branches in San Francisco, Seattle, Phoenix, and Salt Lake City. The following year, we were operating in all eleven western states, and were poised to go nationwide.

By the time Golden Coast hit its five-year mark, not only were we covering all of California like we had originally hoped, but we were performing work in all 50 states with offices in Kansas City, Dallas, Chicago, and Columbus, Ohio. All this growth also meant it was time for a name change, and in order to more accurately reflect the larger scale of our company, Golden Coast became US-Reports, Incorporated.

Because of the lawsuit, US-Reports was years ahead of schedule, and was doing better than Ginger and I had ever anticipated. In fact, we were positioning to become the number one company of our kind in the world. Had it not been for this unexpected lawsuit, we would have remained perfectly content to remain in California, and we never would have become players on the world stage.

Meanwhile, the lawsuit dragged on year after year. Finally, after seven years of hearings, being chased down by process servers, and struggling through many other time-consuming, morale-sapping challenges, I told our attorneys that I simply wanted to settle. Although I still felt the entire lawsuit was carried out against us for both personal and vindictive reasons, I was willing to pay much more than I thought right to end the whole charade.

I typed up a letter outlining the criteria and the final settlement offer, and faxed it to my attorney—or so I thought. In reality, I had accidentally sent it to the opposing counsel. Even so, the transparency of it all was exactly what was needed to bring both sides to the table, and finally, after more than seven years and over a million dollars spent, the struggle was over.

By that time, we had learned the value of persevering through adversity and staying true to what we believe in, regardless of how difficult that may be. We knew that the messages spoken to us by our hearts years earlier were instances of divine communication. Even though it was difficult, and at times my faith wavered, we continued to press forward, and as Ginger so wisely reminded me throughout the lawsuit, things really did work out for our good.

Acting with faith, trusting your heart's inspiration, and working hard to see your objectives through are critical components in the foundation of business success.

Have Faith To Act Urgently

After living through the challenges of the lawsuit, and witnessing the way these challenges actually became unbelievably beneficial, I became convinced that there was indeed a grand plan for Ginger and I, and that what we were doing in our business lives was a critical piece in this plan. Ultimately, the challenges we faced were not only part of our progression in business, but were part of our much larger and more significant progression as human beings. These challenges taught us lessons with eternal value, for we are, after all, eternal beings.

One of the critical lessons I learned through this entire ordeal is the importance of doing all we can do, and then trusting God to carry these efforts through to success. In doing our part, it's absolutely critical that we have the faith to act urgently in following the divine revelations our hearts speak to us. Many times we cannot see the final triumph while we're in the fray of battle, and in these times, we must trust God and know that things will ultimately work for our good.

When we urgently and unhesitatingly act on the promptings of our hearts, we demonstrate our faith that what we're doing is in line with God's will for our lives. Our faithful and urgent action then allows God to have a greater hand in these actions.

When God speaks to us in our hearts, it's time to act. God directs us, His children, to do certain things at very specific times in our lives. He has His own timing, and when we learn to trust Him, we can be confident that we are acting in accordance with His timing and His schedule. When we act in accordance with God's timing, we can be assured that things will work out in the long run for our benefit.

Trusting God's timing, however, can be difficult. As human beings, we are so impatient, and we have such limited views. When we were served with the lawsuit only eight months after opening US-Reports, it seemed as if everything was falling apart. In the moment, it was difficult to see beyond this looming obstacle, but after surviving the whole ordeal, it became clear that God was indeed with us the entire time. Although it may have seemed to us like the wrong time to pursue our entrepreneurial dreams, God knew differently. It was precisely the right time for Ginger and I to act, and because we acted urgently on the promptings of our hearts, everything went according to His plan.

Dallin H. Oaks, a leader of the LDS church, once spoke about the importance of matching the timetable by which we conduct our lives with God's divine timetable for us. He began his address by quoting the Old Testament book of Ecclesiastes: "To every thing there is a season, and a time to every purpose under the heaven: A time to be born, and a time to die; a time to plant, and a time to pluck up that which is planted . . . A time to weep, and a time to laugh; a time to mourn, and a time to dance."[4]

This passage is important in pointing out the fact that there are times in life when certain actions are more in line than others with God's will. God has His timetable for our lives, and a full view of His master plan from beginning to end, but He also allows us free will. If, in God's timing, it's a time to weep, we can still choose to laugh, but this action will pull us away from God's plan by removing us from His timetable.

Oaks continued to explain, "In all the important decisions in our lives, what is most important is to do the right thing. Second, and only slightly behind the first, is to do the right thing at the right time. People who do the right thing at the wrong time can be frustrated and ineffective. They can even be confused about whether they made the right choice when what was wrong was not their choice but their timing." After explaining that our actions are most effective and most powerful when they are made to coincide with God's timetable, Oaks concluded by saying, "We cannot have true faith in the Lord without also having complete trust in the Lord's will and in the Lord's timing."[5]

When we act in accordance with God's timing and God's will, we open ourselves up to receive the maximal degree of divine aid, protection, and blessing, and our actions will therefore be most effective. This is why following your heart urgently and without hesitation is so critical. This type of urgency is an act of faithful obedience to the personal revelation given by God, and such faith qualifies you for His blessings.

Because following the personal revelation given by God is so crucial to your growth and success, it's important to learn how to recognize personal revelation when it occurs.

One day, a friend of another faith visited me in my office. Our conversation eventually arrived at the topic of religion, and he asked me if there was anything different between our respective beliefs. I told him that in my opinion we all worship the same God, but there may be some subtle differences in our views on how we as humans communicate with Deity. "For example," I told him, "I believe in personal revelation."

My friend became slightly defensive and informed me that we already have all the revelation we'll ever need in the Bible. I agreed with him that the words of the Bible are certainly important pieces of revelation applicable to all of humanity, but continued to explain that what I was talking about was revelation of a distinctly personal nature; a literal instance of God speaking to an individual human being—one of His sons or daughters—about ideas, questions, or concerns with immediate relevance to that individual's life.

Explaining to my friend the principle of personal revelation was a positive experience for us both. It's my hope that just as my friend was able to learn more about this incredible principle through our conversation, you also gain a better understanding of personal revelation through reading this book.

While personal revelation typically communicates itself as inspired ideas and positive emotions, it's much more than a fleeting thought or an emotional impulse. Personal revelation is potent. It comes in answer to specific prayers and specific questions. It has staying power, and ultimately becomes a personal conviction rather than a momentary feeling.

Concretely and thoroughly defining personal revelation in all its possible nuances is ultimately impossible—it's just too intimate and personal. But the good news is that as you begin praying for guidance and help, and as you begin putting forth an effort to listen for that inner voice of personal revelation, you will become increasingly adept at recognizing it. God will help you understand the specific and deeply personal way He speaks to you.

As you act urgently to follow this divine inspiration, God will continue blessing you with even more personal revelation and guidance. When you walk down the pathways revealed to you by God at the exact moment He directs you to, you allow yourself to walk as closely to Him as possible.

Sometimes you will question the promptings of your heart, and perhaps will not follow through on them. This hesitation will only delay your progress. If Ginger and I had hesitated on leaving our former company to start our own, we may have become so trapped and legally bound to the new corporation that we may have been forced to stay with them. We may have missed out on the business success and personal growth afforded us by founding, growing, and operating US-Reports.

When you act with urgency in following the inspiration of your heart, you demonstrate faith in God and His plan for you. Although you will only be able to see a very limited portion of your life's path at any one time, this type of faithful action allows you to take the next step into the unknown, into the darkness. This is precisely the point at which God will reveal to you the next portion of the path.

Exercising the faith to act with urgency allows you to progress along the path God has prepared for you. With every step you take, your faith in yourself and in God increases, and a new segment of the path will become clear. Learning to trust His timing and put faith in the guidance God gives us are grand lessons to learn, both in life and in business.

Live Well

In dealing with the lawsuit, I quickly learned there were some things in life I simply cannot control. First and foremost, I have no control over the decisions and actions of others. I had no control over the fact that my former employer chose to do what he did. What I could control, though, was my own response to the situation and my personal actions.

To keep me grounded, I focused on living my personal moral code as closely as I possibly could. In a situation working to strip me of independence, this was what I continued to control. I therefore concentrated on treating others the way I would have them treat me. About three years into the lawsuit, I realized after much pondering and praying, that I needed to forgive my enemies and those who wished me harm. As I learned to apply this principle to my life, my ability to love and help others increased. Years later, when some of my own employees left my company to start businesses of their own, I always wished them well as long as they were sure to uphold the law. Living this way allowed me to avoid having to ever relive the bleak and draining experience of vindictive lawsuits that Ginger and I had already endured, and has become a key to our business success.

Looking back on this experience, I now realize that focusing on the only area I had real control over—my personal actions—not only helped give me a much-needed sense of control in my life, but by ensuring that these actions were in accordance with the moral laws of God, it also allowed me to receive great blessings of divine guidance and aid.

Choosing to make our actions coincide with our personal moral codes has allowed Ginger and I to receive many powerful blessings from Heaven. Although these blessings haven't removed challenges and obstacles from our lives, they have helped us survive and grow from them while continuing to press on toward success.

The Cycle Of Divine Guidance

Looking back over our life in business, we have recognized a cycle that has consistently helped us in our efforts. In fact, following this cycle is the foundation upon which our business achievements have been built, and the same success we've enjoyed is there for anyone else who is willing to follow the steps outlined below.

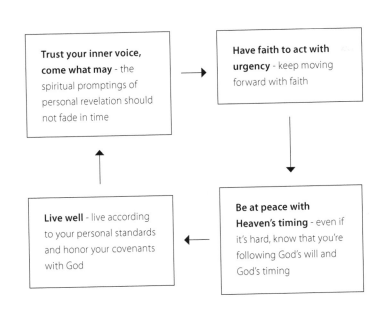

Each component of this cycle directly impacts and builds upon the others. When you receive an impression to do something, recognize this as personal revelation from God, and trust that what your heart is telling you is correct. Such a recognition will help you exercise the faith necessary to follow through and act on these promptings with urgency—keep in mind that as you do so, trials will most likely arise somewhere along the line. When they do, continue to have faith that things will work out, knowing that your life is being lived according to God's will and God's timing. Trust that He can see further than you can; press forward with faith and make lemonade. Finally, in all you do, be sure to live your life well. Living an honest, upright life dedicated to serving others will lead to even greater spiritual sensitivity and guidance, at which point the cycle starts all over again.

Application and Relevance:

1. Find answers to your important questions in the most sacred place you know, be it a chapel, synagogue, temple, sanctuary, or your bedroom. I went to an LDS temple, but what's important is to find a location sacred to you where you feel especially connected to Deity.

2. Follow the promptings of your inner voice. You may not know until later why you have been moved toward a particular path, but trust in divine purpose and the answers will eventually come.

3. The challenges of life, especially in business, often present lessons that will propel your success later on. It's OK to ask questions, but never question the deep and abiding impressions of your heart—these are personal revelations from God.

4. Trust in God's timing.

5. Most importantly, live according to the moral codes and values you know to be true.

Chapter 02

The Power Of Covenants

'"Our deepest fear is not that we are inadequate. Our deepest fear is that we are powerful beyond measure. It is our light, not our darkness that most frightens us.' We ask ourselves, Who am I to be brilliant, gorgeous, talented, fabulous? Actually, who are you not to be? You are a child of God. Your playing small doesn't serve the world. There's nothing enlightened about shrinking so that other people won't feel insecure around you. . . . We were born to make manifest the glory of God that is within us. It's not just in some of us; it's in everyone. And as we let our own light shine, we unconsciously give other people permission to do the same. As we're liberated from our own fear, our presence automatically liberates others."

- Marianne Williamson[6]

Chapter 2 image - A journey worth taking is always to arrive home.

Covenants 101

The path provided by God for our lives—business and otherwise—reveals itself only when we have enough faith to live our personal standards and keep our covenants. Whether Christian or Jew, Muslim or undecided believer, the covenants we make with God, when fulfilled, will light the path before us and connect us to Heaven.

The term "covenant" has several meanings. It may simply be an agreement, usually a formal one, between two or more persons stipulating some specific action and any associated consequences. It may be an incidental clause within an agreement. From a religious perspective, it's a solemn agreement between members of a church to act together in living and maintaining a particular belief system. Biblically speaking, a covenant is a conditional promise made between humanity and God. In these types of covenants, God fixes the terms of the agreement and individuals use their free will to either accept or reject them. For example, the Old Testament outlines the agreement made between God and the Israelites, in which God promised to protect them if they kept His law and were faithful to Him. For the purposes of this book, these are the types of covenants we'll focus on.

I understand that if you've never entered into a covenant with God before, this may be a very unfamiliar and new concept. As you continue reading, however, it will become clear exactly how this principle may be connected to your own belief system in such a way that will bring you greater success in all facets of your life.

Like the ancient Hebrews, people of faith have consistently been taught that if they faithfully live according to the principles and laws of God, such as those contained in the Ten Commandments, they will receive blessings for their obedience. Such blessings generally appear as the natural outcome of these obedient actions.

As an example, it's a fairly simple concept that if we obey the commandment to have no other gods before the true God of Heaven, we won't have room in our spiritual lives to allow the obsessive worship of money or any other worldly thing to creep in, simply because we've already devoted ourselves to a particular spiritual lifestyle. The blessing of keeping this commandment, then, arises as a naturally occurring consequence of our obedience. In this case, following the command to have no other god before God enables us to avoid greed and the dangers of materialism and self-centeredness. As we live according to spiritual laws such as this, and experience firsthand the blessings of this obedience, we gain increased faith in the efficacy of faithful and obedient living.

Often times, within the setting of organized religion, covenants with God will be entered into through public acts such as a baptism or Bar Mitzvah. Other times, commitments to God are made privately through prayer and meditation. Whether public or private, the principle of making and keeping covenants with God is always real, and provides great opportunities for happiness and success in our lives.

In one of my favorite passages of scripture, we learn of a people who successfully kept the commandments of God, which they had agreed to do through making covenants with Him. The passage concludes by inviting us to "consider on the blessed and happy state of those that keep the commandments of God. For behold, they are blessed in *all things, both temporal and spiritual*" (emphasis added).[7]

As this passage makes clear, there is a direct link between success and happiness in our lives—both temporally and spiritually, financially and personally—and living the covenants we have made with God.

At this point, you may be asking, "How do I make a covenant with God? Have I already done so without really knowing I had? What does this process entail, and why is it so important?"

To answer these questions, I want you to think back to a time when you had an intense one-on-one conversation with a parent who was trying to teach you something or convince you to behave in a certain way. I vividly remember a time when my brother lied to my Mom. Back then, things were different, and although my Mom was always a loving and caring woman, the popular modes of discipline may sound a little harsh today. After my brother lied, Mom put cayenne pepper in his mouth and while his tongue was blazing asked him, "Will you ever lie to me again?" Of course, he sputtered out a frantic, "No!"

While this experience certainly had an impact in how my brother chose to behave in the future, the agreement reached between my Mom and my brother is not a covenant. It may have been a powerful lesson leading to a strong personal commitment on the part of my brother, but it was not a true covenant.

A covenant we enter into with God is done so without fear or threat; it is made out of respect, love, and understanding. It is entered into freely and without coercion. A covenant with God is a promise that literally binds an individual to God. Essentially, an individual promises to live according to God's principles and God promises that individual blessings for doing so.

As an example of how covenants work, let me describe some of the duties I perform as a member of the board of directors at a local bank. As a member of the loan committee, I help evaluate the strength of an individual or company to repay any loan we may give them. When we feel that an individual is capable of repaying a loan, we set the terms of the agreement. The potential receiver of the loan then chooses whether or not to accept these terms. If they're agreed to, then the money is loaned and it's up to the receiver to pay back the loan according to the terms of the agreement. As long as that person lives up to his end of the deal, he enjoys the blessings of having the money he needs. If he fails to keep his part of the agreement, however, he is penalized, and thus fails to enjoy the full potential benefit of the loan.

Covenants operate in much the same way. God sets the terms of a covenant. He dictates what is required of an individual in order to receive certain blessings. When a person chooses to enter into a covenant, he or she accepts God's terms. In entering a covenant, it's important to make known your intentions to do so; this is a deeply personal matter. Depending on your level of spirituality, you may seal your commitment to God through a personal prayer of conviction or a more formalized sacred ritual such as baptism.

The key to all this is to understand that after you enter into a covenant with God, you will be held responsible for how well you live according to the morals, values, and spiritual knowledge available to you. As you grow spiritually, you will be held to more exacting standards, and will therefore feel yourself growing even closer to God. After entering into a covenant with God, it's up to you to follow His teachings. When you do this, you'll be blessed. During those times of life, however, when you fail to live according to your covenants, you won't receive these blessings. Of course, keeping your end of a covenant doesn't guarantee an easy and carefree life, but it does guarantee a nearness to God and His spirit of love and comfort that will provide the strength to survive life's tough times.

Throughout all my study of scripture, I have never found anything that explicitly discusses the details regarding how an individual or a society became prosperous, or conversely, how they lost it all. Nowhere have I discovered passages discussing the real-world, dollars-and-cents practices or business techniques of prosperous people.

What is repeatedly made clear, however, is that as long as people are obedient to God's laws and their covenants with Him, they are successful and happy. In the Old Testament, God led the Israelites to the Promised Land and according to their faithfulness in maintaining their covenants to obey His commandments, helped them establish themselves as a mighty nation.

In the New Testament, Paul teaches that "whatsoever a man soweth, that shall he also reap." Because "he that soweth to the Spirit shall of the Spirit reap life everlasting," it is critical for us to "not be weary in well doing."[8]

The Book of Mormon relates the story of an ancient group of people traveling from Jerusalem to the Americas. They, like their Hebrew ancestors before them, became prosperous in their new Promised Land only when they honored their covenants to obey God and His commandments.

God's children have always been the happiest and most prosperous when they obey God's commands, when they make and honor their covenants with Him. This is an important concept to understand and apply to your life as you work toward achieving your business and financial goals, and it's one that I have come to value through firsthand experience.

Early in my life, I was taught the value of keeping the Sabbath Day holy, and while I readily admit my imperfection in fully living this law, I do strive to make Sunday a different and sacred day. As I have tried to set this day aside from all the other busy days of the week, I have been blessed with a sense of renewal that comes from using this one day each week to focus on spiritual and other personal matters rather than business and financial concerns. This in turn reinvigorates me and prepares me to work hard and meet the challenges of the coming week.

The power of keeping the Sabbath Day holy has also been attested by prominent public figures such as Bill Child, who refused to open his stores on Sunday[9], and Senator Joe Lieberman, who does not perform labors on the Sabbath, which for him begins at sundown Friday evening and lasts until sundown of the next day.[10]

In discussing this very specific principle of the Sabbath, what is most important is the larger concept of obedience, and more specifically, obedience within the context of covenant making and keeping. Because I covenanted with God to set aside one day each week to focus on spiritual rather than secular concerns, I am blessed when I honor this promise. My business success is the result of making covenants with God and trying my best to uphold my end of these promises. I, of course, am not perfect in this, but through sustained effort, I believe God has blessed me and helped guide me down the path leading to entrepreneurial success.

You may be wondering if it can really be that simple—if a person honors their covenants with God, will they really be blessed in their business and career pursuits? Because I have experienced it myself, I am living proof that God will not only bless you in your business life, but in all aspects of your personal life as well, when you make and keep covenants with Him.

It's important to note that keeping covenants doesn't provide automatic success, or even easy success. Hard work is still required. Challenges will still arise. But as you make and keep covenants with God, you will be happy regardless of what's going on around you. This is because obedience moves you one step closer to God, the source of all happiness.

The Pipeline To Heaven's Blessings

I've always been intrigued by farming. Growing up in northern Wyoming, I was raised on the land, and it's still in my blood. Fortunately, through some of our other business ventures, Ginger and I have been able to own some fully operating farms, and I've learned a great deal from our work with them.

There was one particular farm that stands out as especially meaningful. In our first year of owning this farm, the corn had already been planted, and it was time to turn on the first water. For some reason, though, there was not enough water pumping through the underground pipes to pressurize and move the sprinkler pivot around the field. The sun was beating down on the young and tender two-inch tall corn shoots. They needed water badly and time was of the essence.

After some investigation, it was discovered that the main line between the pond and the pivot was broken. The previous landowner had not taken care of the pipeline: it wasn't buried deep enough, and it wasn't even the proper type of piping. Given these problems, it's a miracle these fields had begun to sprout at all.

We acted as quickly as we possibly could to fix these problems, yet it still took two weeks before the corn was able to receive adequate watering. Finally, a new pipeline was installed using crush-proof, ten-inch pipe rather than the previously installed flimsy four-inch pipe, and buried at a depth of eight feet rather than the original three or four. This new pipeline was installed carefully and properly, and it immediately allowed a strong and constant flow of water to be carried from the pond to the desperately thirsty corn. Although these setbacks gave us a dangerously late start on the growing season, with the new pipeline in place, we managed to grow a decent corn crop for cattle feed that year.

This experience very clearly illustrates to me the importance of keeping our covenants as it relates to our business activities. As farmers, we hope to grow things of value in our fields, and we understand that the only way this is possible is if our fields are watered. Water is the essential ingredient; it's what makes things grow; it's the stuff of success. The pipeline, then, becomes critical because it provides a direct link between the pond and the field, and allows for the flow of this invaluable water.

In our professional, personal, and entrepreneurial ventures, it's critical that we receive divine guidance and aid: these are as central to your success as water is to the farmer's. In this sense, covenants serve as your personal pipeline, providing a direct link to Heaven, the source of all guidance and blessings.

As made clear in my farming experience, it's not enough to simply have a pipeline in place. If it's not the right kind of piping, if it's not buried deep enough, or if it's not properly maintained, the flow of water will be restricted and the purpose for having a pipeline will be destroyed.

This is why honoring your covenants through obedience to God is absolutely essential. It's not enough to simply talk about covenants or to claim a faith that doesn't lead to action. Covenants become powerful when they lead to genuine belief and action. Only by living an honest, upright, charitable life—a life focused on following your personal moral code—will your pipeline to Heaven be properly maintained. This creates a clear pathway for divine guidance and aid to flow into your life, blessing you in your business, entrepreneurial, and all other meaningful efforts.

Just as crops need water to grow, our entrepreneurial, professional, and other life efforts need divine guidance and aid to succeed.

Covenants are our pipelines to Heaven. Install and maintain the proper pipeline by making covenants with God and honoring them through obedience and moral living.

Like the harvested cornfield, our business and personal ventures will become fruitful through sustained efforts at keeping our covenants.

Final Thoughts

One of the most difficult things I faced while buried in the seven-year lawsuit described in Chapter 1 was the realization that I couldn't always trust and depend on other people. There were times when I watched as associates whom I knew from the past lied on the witness stand simply because they were being paid to represent those suing me. I've always been a fairly trusting individual, so witnessing all this was a very hard thing to deal with.

This aspect of the lawsuit was both a curse and a blessing: realizing the unreliability and untrustworthiness of human beings was painful, yet it ultimately forced me to depend more on God. By the end of the seven year lawsuit, I was determined that regardless of the odds and challenges stacked up against me, I would trust in God and let events unfold as they may. Like the Old Testament prophet Elisha who, when facing the powerful army of Syria, urged his people to "fear not: for they that be with us are more than they that be with them," I believed that if I lived according to what I knew to be right and kept my covenants with God, He would always be on my side to guide, help, and protect me.[11]

The key is to make and keep covenants with God. When we uphold our end of the promise, we can trust that God—who is perfect—will most certainly uphold His. Although it won't always be easy or according to our personal timetables, God will provide a way for us to accomplish the righteous endeavors of our hearts, especially when it comes to our business, financial, career, and entrepreneurial activities.

Covenants →	**Obedience** →	**Trust In God**
Make covenants with God to tap into the source of divine guidance and aid	Keep your pipeline flowing by fulfilling your covenants and living what you know	With your pipeline secure, trust God—He sees the big picture and will direct your path

Application and Relevance:

1. Your inner voice of divine inspiration and guidance can speak to you only when you live your covenants.

2. Obeying God and living according to your moral code is the way to uphold and honor your covenants with God.

3. Trust in God. When we make and keep covenants with Him, He will help fight our battles and guide us with increased inspiration.

4. Remember: One plus God is enough!

Chapter 03

Beware The Double Life

"No man can serve two masters: for either he will hate the one, and love the other; or else he will hold to the one, and despise the other. Ye cannot serve God and Mammon."

- Matthew 6:24

Chapter 3 image - *We cannot walk along two paths, but each day must choose one or the other.*

The idea that our business lives and our personal lives are two entirely separate parts of who we are and how we act is, unfortunately, a very common one. All too often, we talk about "leaving work at work," or attempt to keep our personal lives "at home." Of course, there are times when we check our business concerns at the door in order to more fully focus on what's going on at home with our families, but what I'm really referring to is the more general and fundamental attitude that our business and personal lives are and should be kept separate from one another, and the belief that these two lives will never meet or significantly impact each other.

This idea is a deceiving one, and failing to understand that who we are at work and who we are at home are deeply interconnected will become an obstacle to achieving your entrepreneurial and career goals. On the other hand, striving to be consistent in the way you make decisions and the type of person you are, whether at work or at home, will become a significant benefit to you in your business ventures.

No Duplicity

A tragic example of the way our business and personal lives impact each other involves a former employee of mine who was addicted to pornography. This man, although a talented and hard worker, was ultimately fired because his personal problems began seriously interfering with his business pursuits.

On a visit to the home office, his laptop stopped working, and when Information Technology looked into it, they discovered that the computer had crashed because of numerous viruses picked up at pornographic websites. This damage to company property, combined with his past attempts to use business trips and meetings with other sales representatives as opportunities to act "manly" and visit strip clubs, made him not only an ineffective employee, but a liability to the company as well. When we confronted him about his problems, the way it was affecting his work, and our decision to let him go, he cried like a baby. The whole dilemma was difficult for everyone involved.

This man's story makes clear just how strongly our personal lives intersect with and impact our business lives. What many would consider a personal problem regarding pornography spilled over into his business life to the extent that he began wasting company time and resources in order to satisfy his personal addictions.

This is a sad example of what can happen when a person attempts to live a duplicitous life. Had he been focused on living consistently, regardless of where he was or who he was with, the entire situation could have been avoided. It is nothing more than self-deceit to think you can be one person at home and someone totally different at work. How you behave and who you try to be in one place will always have an effect on who you are and how you act in the other.

In both business and everyday living, the same principles of professionalism, courtesy, and respect are critical, although we may use different words to describe these values when practiced in different settings. For example, in business we try to establish a "community of associates," and we may talk about "taking the high road" of ethical integrity.

When it comes to our activities at home, we focus on these same things, even though we often think and talk about them differently. Away from business, we often focus on being a "good neighbor" or becoming a "nurturing parent." We may be interested in finding ways to "volunteer" or take part in "community service projects." In all these endeavors, the focus is really the same. In the end, the oft-repeated commandment to "love thy neighbour as thyself" applies equally to business associates, family members, friends, acquaintances, and even strangers, and should guide our actions at home, in business meetings, and at the neighborhood barbecue.[12]

This truth is universal and unchanging; it cannot be separated or compartmentalized based upon circumstance. As quoted above, the scriptures make it very clear that we are to treat others with respect and honesty regardless of who that other person is or what's going on around us.

If we carry this logic to its conclusion, we will discover that just as truth cannot change because of circumstance, neither can we if we are striving to live upright and truly successful lives. Once we decide to live according to the commandments of God, and to honor our covenants with Him, we are bound to follow these guidelines in all aspects of our lives. In fact, living this way entirely does away with the belief that we can somehow live two separate lives. When we choose to follow God, we commit ourselves to following His teachings in all places and in all times.

Truly, there can be no duplicitous living if you desire the type of divine guidance and blessing we've discussed in the preceding two chapters. I hope you now have a deeper understanding of the great principle taught by Jesus when He said it's impossible to serve two masters.[13]

To maximize your entrepreneurial and career potential, it's crucial that you decide what type of person you want to become (remember, your relationship with God and the power of making and keeping covenants with Him should help define this person), and then strive to become that person everywhere you are.

It's A Family Affair

Because it's ultimately impossible to separate business life from personal life, it's important to recognize the need for cooperation between your business ventures and your family, and more specifically, your spouse or life partner.

The role of spouses and life partners in business is another area in which people often feel the need to create some sort of division. In 2011, I attended a conference in which a client spoke about his recent international business trips. He mentioned that his wife accompanied him on his travels, and quickly explained that this was okay because his wife also worked in a related field and was very adept at working in public settings. His need to provide some reason for his wife's presence amused me, and I thought, "We don't need excuses for our spouses to come on these journeys do we? My wife accompanies me often because we're a team and we enjoy being together."

Allowing your spouse or partner to become your entrepreneurial and career teammate is key in pursuing your goals and dreams. If you think about any positive and loving relationship in your life, you will recognize that both you and your loved one bring gifts and talents to the relationship that the other person either needs or can learn from. A healthy relationship is one in which both parties freely share their unique abilities, strengths, and attributes so that both people can learn, grow, and become better together.

For this reason, it's critical that both members of a relationship are given equal opportunities to speak, make suggestions, and contribute. Too often, one half of the relationship equation becomes a subordinate, and when this happens, "unrighteous dominion" occurs.[14] That is to say, one partner becomes the dominant bully and the other believes he or she must become submissive to the will of the bully in order to maintain peace. Roles are established early on in a relationship, and if they're established through this type of bullying method, it will result in severe and perhaps eternal damage to the relationship—this is just bad business!

We all have the need for recognition, appreciation, and respect. When both parties of a relationship are equal members, able to share their talents and unique personalities freely, confident in the feeling that they're contributing to the overall success of the partnership, all these needs are met.

By allowing your spouse to become involved with your business affairs, contributing ideas and providing feedback, praise, and constructive criticism, you create a constant support system for one another. This will deepen the affection you feel for each other, and will help establish a unique equality that can't be achieved in any other way.

With that said, don't feel that it's necessary for your spouse to become a legally recognized and official business partner. If this works for you and your business, that's great, but it's not absolutely essential. What is important, however, is that you allow your life partner to become as involved as possible. Let him or her feel free to share ideas, suggestions, and input. Talk with each other about what's going on with your work, and as you do, you will find in your spouse an invaluable teammate providing consistent support and encouragement.

A key concept to remember in all this is transparency, a principle taught particularly well in Stephen M.R. Covey's *The Speed of Trust*.[15] Being forthright and honest in our domestic partnerships, including complete transparency in all things, is paramount. Let me share an example that may seem somewhat trivial, but which clearly illustrates why transparency with spouses and life partners regarding business activity is important.

I once inspected a large complex in Long Beach, California. In the basement were somewhere around 100 blue, stainless steel soda acid fire extinguishers. They were old and were no longer legal to use as active extinguishers, and so had been removed to the basement. As I stared at these fire extinguishers—worthless clutter to the company I was inspecting—I had visions of a hundred nice, shiny, gorgeous lamps. I offered to take the extinguishers off the building owner's hands, free of charge. He wanted a hundred bucks and I obliged. So, without consulting my wife and partner, I stuffed as many of these old fire extinguishers as I could into our family station wagon and brought them home, ready to lovingly convert each one into a lamp. You can imagine the conversation that ensued when I finally got home, and Ginger saw how much of our living room these extinguishers took up.

We did eventually make them into nice lamps, took them to the swap meet, and sold two—that's right—two. My beautiful fire extinguisher lamps quickly became gifts for many weddings and birthdays—who wouldn't want a fire extinguisher lamp, right?

Looking back on this experience, the importance of involving our spouses and life partners in our business decisions with complete transparency is clear. Had I consulted with my partner first, this poor and fruitless decision could have been avoided altogether, and many people could have been spared receiving some strange birthday presents.

I learned that my bright ideas should not operate in a vacuum, especially if that vacuum is the one sitting on my shoulders. Instead, ideas should be shared with our confidants, and if we involve our spouses or life partners in our business affairs, talking to them about our business ideas, career goals, and financial dilemmas with full transparency, they will become our most trusted and supportive teammates.

In his book, *The Five Dysfunctions of a Team*, Patrick Lencioni uses a pyramid to outline the way that a lack of trust between partners eventually leads to failure:[16]

Inattention to
Results

Avoidance of
Accountability

Lack of
Commitment

Fear of
Conflict

Absence of
Trust

Using Lencioni's pyramid as an outline of how to handle business decisions, let's take another look at my extinguisher lamp experience, and imagine what I should have done differently. Beginning at the pyramid's base, to achieve successful results I would have needed to demonstrate enough trust in my partner to reveal my plan to her before buying the fire extinguishers. This communication would have led to a healthy debate or discussion, after which a decision with mutual buy-in would have been made. Because the decision would be made together, we would have both been fully committed and accountable in making sure our decision was successfully carried out. In the end, the accountability brought about through mutual decision-making and commitment would have led to the best possible results.

As attested by its poor commercial reception, my lamp idea was a bad one. This was a business plan that never should have seen the light of day, and had I been open with my partner, communicating with her in full transparency, it never would have progressed beyond the initial brainstorming phase. Luckily this was only a small and mostly inconsequential business scheme, but the lesson it illustrates still holds true: Involving your spouse or life partner in your business ideas and concerns helps create a partnership of trust and support that will help you avoid pitfalls and focus your energy on the most meaningful activities.

Putting It All Together

I have come to believe the underlying foundation of business success is trust. In Chapter 2, we taught that the number one thing a person can do to achieve success in life is to live the covenants they've made with God. This is, in reality, a principle centered on trust. If God can trust you to be one who strives to live a life in accordance with covenants and promises you have made to Him and to others, and you learn to be equally trustworthy and transparent in your dealings with business and life partners, then you have a great chance of success in your professional adventures.

Howard Ruff, a very successful businessman in his day, wrote: "Without the support of your spouse, starting a new business is next to impossible."[17] If you don't have full and open trust, communication, cooperation, agreement, buy-in, and mutual respect in your marriage or life partnership, your business and entrepreneurial efforts will lack the foundation of support needed for success.

The key to this type of supportive life relationship is open communication. Be completely transparent in all facets of life, and keep in mind that things change. As they do, it's critical to maintain an open line of communication between yourself and your spouse. This will ensure that you're both working together in full cooperation toward the same ultimate goals.

As Ginger and I have focused on being open and honest with each other, we've been able to support one another through the ebbs and flows of life. We've learned how to allocate our efforts, ideas, and skills in the most effective ways. For example, when our children were having problems at school, Ginger had to temporarily step away from her heavy involvement in the day-to-day operations of the company. During this time, we communicated openly and kept each other fully aware of what was going on; I knew what the kids' needs were and she knew what the company's needs were. By supporting each other and working together, we made it through this challenging time. Although we had different duties and responsibilities, we were still on the same team, working toward the same goal.

The only way to develop and maintain the type of support necessary for success is to live a consistently honest and forthright life. Avoid the temptation to try living two separate lives. Be transparent and trustworthy in your interactions with business partners, clients, your spouse, and with God. The duplicitous life makes this impossible, and such a lifestyle will eventually catch up to you with disastrous outcomes.

I have found that the idea of being equally yoked with one's spouse when it comes to career and entrepreneurial endeavors typically resonates with people when they begin thinking about it. This is because it's right. After teaching this principle as part of a training program for young entrepreneurs in New Zealand, a participant emailed me. In his letter, he wrote:

Thank you so much for spending time with us at the Launching Leaders graduation weekend, it was an absolute delight to have had the privilege to converse with you and your wife. . . . You and your wife make a great team and I hope and pray that I too may be so blessed to find someone like [Ginger]. Someone who will help me as I begin to embark on my financial adventures as your wife has helped you through these years. . . . [I will] email you for future advice when I come to important business decisions in the future.

Much love and appreciation,

Yi-Han Wu

As expressed in his letter, Yi-Han was fascinated as he learned about the husband–wife connection within the context of business success. What I was hoping to express at Yi-Han's conference, and what I hope I'm expressing now, is that when we find our soul-mate/spouse/life partner, why wouldn't we want to involve him or her in all the details of our life? Why would we want to separate that person from this part of ourselves and begin to compartmentalize the relationship by not involving them?

A few months after his first email, Yi-Han wrote back:

So my question for you is: How crucial is it that when one seeks a spouse one considers how compatible their goals and ambitions are? . . . Or is it possible to simply have the husband take care of all the business, investments, and money, and still be able to achieve something great?

Of course, it's possible for one person to handle the business and financial aspects of a marriage or partnership and for that relationship to still find success. The question is, though, is this the best practice? My experience says, "Definitely not." Just because something isn't bad doesn't mean it's necessarily the best, and if we were to judge the principle of conducting business in full cooperation and transparency with one's spouse, it will always rank best.

In my experiences as an entrepreneur I have worked with many different people. I have seen partners and spouses who literally pulverize each other in public business quarrels. I have also seen partners and spouses who show immense respect for each other at all costs. The difference in the level of success of these two groups, in terms of business accomplishments and the strength of their relationships is immense, with the latter group always coming out on top.

Application and Relevance:

1. You can't have two sets of standards; your personal and business lives must be congruent.

2. Business and careers are a family enterprise.

3. Consider your spouse or life partner your number one advocate and source of strength. Living a consistently honest and transparent lifestyle, rather than a duplicitous one, allows you to create this trusting and supportive relationship.

4. Decide that trust is the best foundation from which to build success, and live in such a way that business partners, life partners, and God can all trust you to consistently do the right thing.

5. Great ideas should be shared and discussed, not thrust upon others.

6. Imagine the joy that can exist when there are no secrets between partners.

7. Use these questions to assess how well you're doing in building a relationship of trust and transparency with your spouse or life partner:

    a. Do I esteem my business acumen as superior to my spouse/life partner?

    b. Do I talk over my partner in others' presence either to establish superiority or to "protect" my partner from saying something that might appear non-sensible?

    c. Do I withhold vital information, especially financial information, from my spouse/life partner?

    d. Do I embrace and recognize the contributions of my spouse/life partner with grace and appreciation?

    e. When I am not with my spouse/life partner, do I miss them? Do I act differently?

    f. Do I seek for the praises of others over the genuine affections of my spouse/life partner?

Beware The Double Life **83**

Chapter 04

The Formula And Happiness

"Controlling your life means controlling your time. By mastering this, you will have taken complete control of your own life, your own destiny, and you will have a right to this magnificent thing that no one can take away from you called inner peace."

- Hyrum W. Smith[18]

Chapter 4 image - *The heights we wish to climb are always achieved by steadiness and hard work.*

I remember well the years when Ginger and I were newly married and living in Simi Valley, California. Our first child had just been born, and we worked hard to support our growing little family. I threw the *Los Angeles Times* from 2 a.m. to 6 a.m., came home for an hour-long nap and a quick breakfast, and then headed off again to work selling vacuum cleaners to stores and other established vendors. For date nights, we walked to the nearest 7-Eleven, purchased a Big Gulp with two straws, and walked through the park sharing our drink. This was all we could afford at the time, but we look back on these days as wonderful and sweet.

It was also during this period of our lives that we met some of the most influential individuals we've ever known; people who taught us invaluable life lessons without which we never would have found the success we now enjoy.

One Sunday, while attending our local church congregation, a new family arrived. The parents were in their mid- to late-thirties and they had seven children. James and Carolyn Ritchie were so positive and filled with life that Ginger and I became determined to get to know them better. We discovered that they lived just up the hill from us, and they immediately agreed to our coming over to visit. As we got to know them better, we learned that James had retired from running his many businesses at the age of 35 and that he and his wife had decided to devote the rest of their lives to giving back in the form of church and community service.

Ginger and I were shocked. The Ritchies weren't that much older than us, and here we were, struggling to pay for cloth diaper service, and he had already retired! I wanted to know how that was possible.

My curiosity soon led to a special friendship that I often compare to that of Mr. Miyagi and Daniel Larusso in the 1984 film *The Karate Kid*. Every Saturday morning, I would arrive at the Ritchie's home to have a chat with my self-adopted mentor, my personal Mr. Miyagi. As James sat in his Winnebago reading the newspaper, he would eventually pause what he was reading, look over the top of the paper through his glasses, give me a little morsel of advice and send me on my way. "Go read *The Richest Man in Babylon* and come back to discuss it."[19] And so I did . . .

This pattern continued for some time. Finally, when he felt I was ready, James shared "The Formula" with me. In time, as Ginger and I have worked to follow the principles of The Formula, the things it teaches has changed our lives forever. We now feel that The Formula is perhaps the greatest, most concise, and most clear guide for living a successful life. The Formula is a concept I believe in with my whole heart, because as we began living by it, we realized that our Heavenly Father's designs for us are much more than we can ever imagine. We began understanding that our potential is limitless, and that we are all fully capable of controlling our lives and embarking on the pathways of our Divine potential.

As I look back on the early days of our relationship with the Ritchies, I am grateful that someone believed in us and loved us enough to share not only a sense of hope, but a concrete way to realize our hopes and dreams as well. For hope without a plan is much like an airplane without an engine: it may look really nice, but until it's airborne, it's not really achieving the true purpose of its creation. With the help of The Formula, Ginger and I were able to glimpse what we were capable of becoming, and then set out to achieve it.

Since our adoption of The Formula and its associated principles, we have, in a time of great economic uncertainty, created a life wherein we can devote significant time and resources to pursuing those things we care most about in our lives. We have the financial security to cover whatever we need, and then some. We have truly seen the principles of The Formula work in our lives, helping us achieve entrepreneurial success and financial independence, but The Formula has also taught us just how little we ourselves are responsible for all this. Really, God is responsible for making our successes possible, and it's only by recognizing this and living our lives according to the spiritual principles upon which The Formula is built that we have been able to attain our goals and ambitions.

When James first shared The Formula with me, he said, "If God would allow these principles of success to work on a polio stricken, stuttering, chicken farmer from Heber, Utah (speaking of himself), then why wouldn't He do the same for you?" Now, as you begin reading and learning about The Formula, I echo this same question: If a self-educated farm boy who, along with his wife, was able to make a significant mark for good in the world as a result of implementing the principles of The Formula, why wouldn't God do the same for every single person willing to learn and apply these same principles to his or her life?

For both the Ritchies and us, the final proof of The Formula's efficacy came 20 years after James first shared it with me. James and Carolyn were then serving without pay as directors of the Willes Center for International Entrepreneurship at Brigham Young University—Hawaii, and Ginger and I, after working hard and finding our own success in the world of business and entrepreneurialism, had been invited to share a presentation at a conference attended by several hundred business students. At the conclusion of our presentation, while pondering his own blessings and successes, the successes experienced by Ginger and I, and the future successes of those in that conference, James leaned back, and with tears streaming down his cheeks, said, "It works; The Formula really works."

In the following section, James shares The Formula in his own words. Please read, enjoy, and absorb this profound teaching as outlined and explained by the man who created it.

James Ritchie: The Formula For Success—The Basics

As mentioned in the previous chapter, trust is really the foundation for any success in life, business and otherwise. Trust is something that permeates all our activities, and affects all aspects of how we live and interact with others. Both Stephen R. Covey and his son, Stephen M.R. Covey, have written historic books and lectured around the world on the principle of trust.[20] We must trust ourselves, others must trust us, and we must find mentors in whom we can trust. All three levels of trust are vital if we are going to not only make it through this divinely inspired obstacle course we call life with confidence and happiness, but ultimately find ourselves at the Pearly Gates when it's all over.

While it's not my intent to repeat what the Coveys have so well documented, I do want to summarize a few of their words of wisdom as an introduction to The Formula. Stephen R. Covey wrote the best seller *The Seven Habits of Highly Effective People*, and these "Seven Habits" have become almost legendary.

Three of these habits are necessary for achieving, on a daily basis, what he calls a "Private Victory:"

1. Be Proactive (the Granddaddy of all habits).

2. Begin With The End In Mind (those who win Private Victories see where they want to end up).

3. First Things First (have a plan, then execute the plan).

Through Private Victories, we learn to trust ourselves. We learn to control our minds, emotions, and appetites. We gain confidence that we are capable of accomplishing greatness in the world.

Along with the habits required for Private Victories, Covey outlines three habits essential in achieving what he calls a "Public Victory:"

1. Think Win/Win (versus Win/Lose, which is the mindset in which most of us grow up).

2. First Seek To Understand, Then Seek To Be Understood (empathetic listening).

3. Create Synergy (1+1 = anything greater than 2).

Public Victories occur when we demonstrate to the world—bosses, work associates, clients, investors—that we are worthy of their trust. In the business marketplace, this type of trust usually translates into revenues and profits. As potential clients and other associates trust us to perform our duties effectively, they will trust us with their business.

The seventh habit exhibited by all highly effective people is that they are constantly "sharpening the saw." That is, they are consistently reading, writing, exercising, eating right, thinking, developing talents, etc. (In fact, since you're reading this book, you're "sharpening the saw" right now.)

Covey, in very few words, captured the essence of his "Seven Habits" with this summary:

Private Victory Precedes Public Victory

The habits of a Private Victory prepare us to trust ourselves before we leave the security of our homes and enter the marketplace, where we all hope to achieve our Public Victories through gaining the trust of all those we work or serve with. Hence, we need to experience regular Private Victories, during which we learn to trust ourselves, before we try to convince the external and public world that we are worthy of their trust.

In many ways, this fundamental message resonates with the teachings of the Bible. In the New Testament, it's important to note that just before Jesus was publicly betrayed, arrested, condemned, and finally crucified, He suffered privately in the Garden of Gethsemane.

After entering this garden alone—"he was withdrawn from [the Disciples] about a stone's cast"—Jesus prayed: "Father, if thou be willing, remove this cup from me: nevertheless not my will, but thine, be done."[21] Immediately following this prayer, we read of his great personal suffering: "And being in an agony he prayed more earnestly: and his sweat was as it were great drops of blood falling down to the ground."[22]

It is significant that this was a challenge endured alone and in private. In many ways, Jesus' victory in the Garden of Gethsemane set the stage for his ultimate—and this time fully public—triumph on the cross at Calvary.

Thus reconsidered in Biblical terms, Covey's basic message reads:

Gethsemane Preceded Calvary

Jesus proved to Himself that He could be trusted in enduring the trials and agonies of the Garden of Gethsemane—this was His Private Victory—and it occurred before He carried the cross to Calvary and won His crowning Public Victory.

Now, as the Bible teaches, we must go and do likewise.[23] We must learn to trust ourselves before we become worthy of the trust of others.

As we strive to become both trusting and trustworthy, I believe it's equally important to have mentors whom we can trust—mentors who will counsel, lead, and be an example in our lives. I have had many mentors in my life, and The Formula has taken shape largely as a result of the combined examples, teachings, and advice of these several mentors. As I consider the crucial roles played by each one, it's clear that the timing and circumstances involved in my meeting and interacting with these individuals are not coincidences, but rather, parts of God's divinely inspired path for me as His child.

The genesis of The Formula occurred on a ferry crossing the River Clyde, just outside of Glasgow, Scotland in October 1964. I was then serving a two-year volunteer ministerial mission, and my mission president—the man overseeing all missionary activity in the region— was David B. Haight, who later became a prominent and well-known leader of the LDS church.

At the time of the ferry ride, I had completed 23 of my 24 months of service, and was preparing to leave Scotland and return home to Utah. President Haight was visiting with me as we leaned against the rail of the ferry, enjoying the afternoon together. Having worked under the leadership of this man for some considerable time, I had learned to trust him wholeheartedly, and to listen to his advice and counsel. As I was then preparing to return home to take on the intimidating worlds of education, marriage, and careers, I was especially keen to follow any advice he had for me.

He said to me (and I memorized every word):

"Go Home, Get Your Education, Make Your Mark, And Get Prepared To Be Of Service."

When I first heard them, these words didn't seem as significant as they were to become later on, as life progressed and I began to really internalize his counsel. On the long flight home from Glasgow to Salt Lake City, his words played over and over in my mind. I slowly began to see the brilliance of this seemingly simple advice, and especially the order in which he had issued each piece of it. As I continued to think, his words took on the shape of a formula that, if followed in the proper order and according to the proper specifications, would yield a final desired result. Here's what this simple formula looks like in greater detail:

1. **Get Your Education:** We must be properly trained and must constantly work to obtain all the wisdom we possibly can. This requires a love for learning and includes both formal, in the classroom training as well as informal, real-world education. Education prepares us to enter the marketplace confidently, fully equipped with the tools needed to become successful in achieving our Public Victories.

2. **Make Your Mark:** We need to make a difference in every community we live in, and in every career opportunity we pursue. We must strive to make our mark a positive one in this world.

3. **Get Prepared To Be Of Service:** These few words made The Formula different from all the other self-help counsel and various formulas for success I had ever heard. Here, I was being counseled with the secrets of eternal success, not just temporal—and therefore, temporary—success. Service and giving back, rather than material wealth and comfort, generate the truest and greatest happiness we can experience in our lives.

Working together, these three components will point any person toward great individual success and lasting happiness. By learning as much as you possibly can—whether from professors, mentors, books, talking to successful individuals, or hopefully a combination of them all—you begin winning the Private Victories of knowledge, organization, preparedness, and confidence. Once you're prepared to enter the marketplace to pursue your Public Victories, it's critical to keep in mind that the ultimate goal is to set yourself up to be of service to others. When this is your focus, you will naturally begin making your mark on the world around you in a positive way.

Striving to make your mark in the world motivates you to become self-reliant, and self-reliance spawns self-confidence. Self-confidence, in turn, will help you reach out to others in need, and when you do this, you will find true happiness and inner peace. Once you have experienced the joys of service, you will find it more difficult to go back into the "real world" of material concerns. You will discover yourself focusing more and more on working to make the world around you better—which, in the end, simply leads you to even greater happiness.

The Formula is incredible in the way each step directly feeds into the next—the more you live one step, the better prepared you are to live the next one. The Formula is strictly positive and constructive—it doesn't rely on manipulation, dishonesty, or exploitation of any kind. Instead, it works to achieve happiness for as many people as possible.

The formula works!

James Ritchie: The Formula For Success— Expanded Principles

The three fundamental principles of The Formula are powerful and effective all on their own, but The Formula actually gets even better. As I became a convert to The Formula, I also read J. Paul Getty's autobiography wherein he outlines his own three-step formula for success:[24]

4. **Get Up Early:** All of my heroes in life have been early risers.

5. **Work Hard:** There's no free lunch—hard work has been a main tenet of every successful person I've ever known.

6. **Find Oil:** At first I thought this was funny—as if we can all just wander outside and strike oil! But when I stopped laughing I saw the wisdom in Getty's third step. Everyone, to be successful, has to build a better mousetrap or provide a superior service to his or her competitor. That product or service then becomes that person's oil.

Now, let's combine this new three-step formula with our original formula, and make a **guaranteed six step formula for happiness:**

1. Get Up Early.
2. Work Hard.
3. Get Your Education.
4. Find Your Oil.
5. Make Your Mark.
6. Get Prepared To Be Of Service.

James Ritchie: A Fairy Tale Life

Let me conclude by relating some important events from my personal life as evidence of The Formula's power. These parts of my life are the result of learning The Formula, and then working overtime to not only incorporate, but to really internalize and buy into the six principles outlined above.

When I got home from Scotland and enrolled at Brigham Young University I continued getting up early and working hard, and took serious the advice to get my education.

Around this same time, I began feeling desires to marry and start a family. In this aspect of my life, I applied the same principles of getting up early and working hard that were becoming such a benefit to my educational pursuits. As I began dating, and women would question why they would want to marry a former chicken farmer from the small town of Heber, Utah, whose childhood battle with polio had left him with a bad leg, and who definitely didn't look anything like Romeo, I would quietly but confidently tell them, "You have correctly identified my physical infirmities and my lack of strikingly good looks, but (at this point, a dramatic pause became a real weapon for success) **I have the formula!**"

Eventually, my persistent hours and hard work in both the classroom and the world of dating paid off, and a beautiful young lady from St. George, Utah decided to take a chance on me. Today, forty-five years later, we have eight wonderful children and thirty-eight brilliant grandchildren—and our family's not finished yet!

Let me finally share with you a broad overview of the challenges and successes I've experienced, and ultimately, the fairy tale life The Formula has motivated and enabled my family and me to live. As this timeline demonstrates, life has been a grand and exciting adventure, and it can become this same type of adventure for anybody willing to work hard to learn and implement the principles espoused in The Formula.

1943: Born to "goodly parents" in Heber City, Utah.[25]

1944: Life and death struggle with polio and five months in the hospital. This battle left me with a permanent limp in my left leg.

1945: Stuttering complications. As a young boy, my difficulties speaking caused some self-esteem issues that I'd have to cope with throughout childhood.

1960: After an operation on my polio-damaged left leg, I developed a serious gangrene infection that nearly led to the amputation of that leg. Before going into the operating room, my father and several neighbors placed their hands on my head and gave me a special blessing, asking God to bless me with health. Miraculously, color returned to my leg, and the infection disappeared. This is a powerful example of God's love, and demonstrated to me the power of faith.

1961: Elected Student Body President of Wasatch High School, despite limping leg and stuttering speech.

1962: Began my church mission in Scotland and met David B. Haight.

1963: While on my mission, I experienced another miracle, as I was able to conquer my stuttering problem. While serving in Scotland, one of the local church leaders invited me to accompany him on his Sunday visits to various congregations. At each of these visits, he delivered powerful sermons, and he always asked me to share a brief message as well. This terrified me, but by being "forced" to stand each week and speak, I gradually found my voice. I slowly developed the confidence to speak, until one day, I finally gave an address that was not filled with stammering and stuttering. This experience was a testament to me of what can happen when a person works hard while maintaining faith in God.

1964: The basics of The Formula shared by David B. Haight on the River Clyde in Glasgow, Scotland.

1966: Married the beautiful Carolyn Orton of St. George, Utah.

1967: Graduated from BYU with a bachelor's degree in Accounting and a minor in Chemistry. I then attended one year of law school at the University of Utah before leaving to pursue entrepreneurial opportunities.

1968-1978: These were the main years in which Carolyn and I began Making Our Mark. We maximized our entrepreneurial aspirations by beginning and developing scores of business ventures. By 1978, when we "retired" from active entrepreneurialism, we were involved in 26 different businesses and companies including Ritchie's Chevrolet, Heber Valley Feed, Ritchie's Ski-doo, Ritchie's International, Valley Pride Credit, Sears Catalog Store, a KOA Campground, Pleasant Valley Trailer Park, Park Place, Leon Acres, St. George Travel Lodge East, Tree House of Blackfoot, Idaho, CRS, E&R Enterprises, a Big O Tire store, Centennial, D&R Enterprises, SLC Enterprises, JoAnn's, Telcondo World Inc., St. George Convention Center, Wasatch Motel, and several others.

1978: Our first retirement at age 35. We then moved our family to California where we volunteered to teach religion classes to local high school students for one year.

1979-1986: Our one year of teaching in California turned into several more years of service, teaching religion classes for students attending UCLA and Moorpark College. During this time I was asked to preside over a collection of LDS congregations, totaling a membership of 2,000 people, in a position known as "Stake President." During this time we also developed several travel agencies and a world travel company.

1986-1989: During this three-year period, we moved to Virginia where we were asked to preside over and supervise more than 600 LDS missionaries serving in the Virginia Roanoke Mission.

1989-94: Came out of retirement to help in phase II of the Franklin Quest launch. During this time the company went public and became a billion dollar corporation. I served as Senior V.P. over sales and training.

1997-99: We accepted a volunteer two-year teaching assignment in New Zealand where we developed an LDS Institute of Religion for college-aged students. The program grew from having 200 enrolled to nearly 700 when we completed our two years of service.

2001-2003: We spent two years presiding over various educational programs of the LDS church in 23 countries throughout southeast Africa.

2004-2006: We were invited to return to Africa for two more years to preside over the LDS church's Missionary Training Center in Ghana.

2008-11: We accepted an invitation to volunteer as the first non-paid directors of the Willes Center for International Entrepreneurship at Brigham Young University—Hawaii.

As evidenced in my life story, The Formula is ultimately a set of principles designed to help anybody who follows them become successful and happy in all aspects of life. Understanding that there can really be no fundamental difference between a person's spiritual life, business life, physical life, or home and family life, these principles must be exercised consistently and at all times. If you allow them to dictate the way you approach your life every single day, you will begin to see great personal growth and you will put yourself on the path toward success and happiness.

The real power of The Formula lies in its spiritual focus on serving others. This represents the greatest distinction between The Formula and the seemingly endless collection of self-help theories and entrepreneurial strategies available in the world. By making this your focus, you will give yourself the tools to do whatever is necessary to reach your own personal goals, but you will act and achieve in such a way that empowers and enables those around you as well. In the end, this is where your greatest happiness awaits.

Application and Relevance:

1. Remember that trust is the foundation of any life success, especially in business.

2. Remember, Private Victories precede Public Victories, or put Biblically, Gethsemane preceded Calvary.

3. Private Victories teach you to trust yourself, and provide the confidence needed to enter the marketplace where you will prove yourself worthy of others' trust.

4. The Formula for success and happiness:

   a. Get Up Early.
   b. Work Hard.
   c. Get Your Education
   d. Find Your Oil.
   e. Make Your Mark.
   f. Get Prepared To Be Of Service

5. True and lasting happiness comes through serving others, and when you aim your personal, career, and entrepreneurial goals in this direction, you will receive the greatest amount of divine guidance, aid, and finally, success.

Chapter 05

The Value Of Strong Mentors

"Mankind was my business. The dealings of my trade were but a drop of water in the comprehensive ocean of my business."

- Charles Dickens[26]

As Ginger can attest, I've always had a hard time doing anything alone. Early in my entrepreneurial career, I attempted to start a business with a partner simply because I was afraid of doing it on my own. This is a horrible reason for doing anything, and from the very beginning this partnership was doomed. I ended up doing 99% of the work necessary to get ready to launch, and only three months later, I bought him out—he just didn't want to put in the hard work needed to get a new business up and running.

This experience taught me a lesson: Choose very carefully who you go into business with, and never become partners with a person just because you're afraid of the unknown.

There are probably many people out there who feel much like I do when it comes to doing things alone. It can be discouraging when partnerships turn out like the one I just described, and we end up feeling more abandoned and alone than ever.

Fortunately for all of us, I'm not going to recommend that we just get over it and learn to work on everything alone. Rather, I've become a firm believer in the need for mentors in our lives—people we can trust and learn from, people we can always rely on. While business partnerships can come and go, begin and end, finding a true mentor will provide an anchor in all your business activities. Mentors will become important people who, through their examples, support, and the lessons they teach, will always be a part of your professional endeavors.

Seek Out And Adopt Mentors

Throughout our formative years of childhood, education, and young adulthood, we generally have several groups of people who surround us with fairly constant support. These people include:

- Parents
- Teachers
- Tutors
- Friends who sincerely care about us
- Church and community leaders

In addition to our relationships with these people, we should always strive to develop and improve our relationships with God. All of these people are mentors to us.

Because these types of mentors are typically around us in one way or another as we grow up, it can be especially intimidating when we try to take the new journey of beginning a career, changing jobs, or becoming an entrepreneur. These journeys are not only entirely new and untried, but most likely the most important ones of our lives as well. When we embark on such journeys, we may suddenly realize that we've never really been on our own before. We find ourselves feeling overwhelmed, and it becomes easy to flounder and give up, retreating to safer ground rather than continuing to labor in the unknown.

The threat of the unknown is especially relevant to entrepreneurs. While many industries have built-in mentorship programs and apprenticeship periods, the lone and dreary world of bootstrapping your own business has very few, if any, of these safeguards already in place. Truly, being in charge of your own business can be one of the loneliest jobs possible. This is why it's important to recognize the need for mentors in our lives, and because such mentors aren't automatically provided, we need to actively seek out and adopt the right types of mentors whenever we can.

The story goes that the young child asked Grandma why the biscuits were burned. She said, "Well, they started to rise, but got burned in the squat." According to this proverbial Grandma, while the biscuit dough was working so hard to rise in order to become the perfect batch of biscuits, the oven's heat became overpowering and the biscuits were ruined.

Many young careers and businesses also get "burned in the squat," meaning they didn't have the chance to rise to proficiency before going out on their own, and were consequently unable to keep up with all the demands of a competitive marketplace.

For Michael E. Gerber, author of *The E-Myth Revisited*, this tendency to get "burned" before achieving an adequate level of proficiency shouldn't necessarily be feared, because it arises from natural weaknesses and limitations found in all of us:

"The fact of the matter is that we all have an Entrepreneur, Manager, and Technician inside us. And if they were equally balanced, we'd be describing an incredibly competent individual. . . . Unfortunately, our experience shows us that few people who go into business are blessed with such a balance. Instead, the typical small business owner is only 10 percent Entrepreneur, 20 percent Manager, and 70 percent Technician."[27]

The difficulties and fears we face as entrepreneurs and professionals are normal, and adopting strong mentors is one of the most effective things we can do to overcome these challenges. Mentors are individuals who have already experienced the challenges of life as a businessperson and who have successfully learned to overcome them. They are people who place great value in sharing their wealth of knowledge, experience, and ideas with others who are striving to work hard to achieve their own successes. A good mentor will care about you as an individual, and will listen to your concerns, questions, and ideas.

The advice mentors provide is invaluable because it's based on real-world experiences. When you listen to your mentors, they will help guide you away from the pitfalls so likely to confront an entrepreneur or businessperson and help you reach your goals of financial and professional success.

Because mentors are such powerful tools in reaching this type of success, it's important to consider what types of people make good mentors, as well as how you will approach these individuals. Here are some tips in finding and adopting good mentors:

- Thoughtfully and prayerfully ponder what types of mentors you need in your life. Consider your goals, your strengths, and especially your weaknesses. Think about what type of person would best help you overcome your challenges and reach your goals.

- With your image of an ideal mentor in mind, be watchful for people who may meet these ideals and who possess these attributes. Have faith that they'll somehow present themselves to you—remember, there are no coincidences.

- Make sure that any potential mentor will raise you to higher ground. This assessment may initially be based on a quick "gut feeling," but as you get to know him or her better, the type of impact this person has on you will become clearer. Run from any potential mentor who doesn't allow you to see yourself in a greater light. Even if a mentor is hard on you, the feeling you should get from working with a mentor should never be demeaning, but always uplifting.

- A great mentor will take an interest in you personally, and will be ready to adopt you for life.

- Mentors should not have a personal financial interest in your success at the outset, and perhaps never throughout your career (although you may become business partners at some point down the road). They should be willing to share their wisdom and knowledge out of a sincere and selfless desire for your betterment rather than for personal financial gain.

- A good mentor–student relationship should become meaningful to both parties.

- Great mentors receive as much joy in your successes as they do their own. They will become some of your greatest cheerleaders, so look for mentors who care about you deeply and who demonstrate an abiding attitude of selflessness.

- Mentors, by definition of being successful professionals, are generally very busy individuals. Yet good mentors should never make you feel like the time they give you is a burden to them.

- Keep in mind that good mentors become friends for life. A mutual interest between mentor and student will develop that brings a greater sense of commitment and dedication to both sides of the relationship.

- When approaching potential mentors, be bold enough to directly ask for some of their time. When they agree, set an appointment and share your goals, ideas, questions, and concerns with them. Find out if they are able and willing to help you achieve these goals. If a potential mentor denies your request, then so be it— move on to someone who's willing to take a sincere interest in you and your goals.

- Always be communicative, clear, and direct when approaching and speaking to potential mentors. Only through candid communication will you find the right person to become your mentor.

Once you've found and adopted strong and uplifting mentors, keep them close for the rest of your life. Be open in sharing your ideas and concerns, and in asking them questions. Mentors who care prepare the path for others to follow. They stay involved, even if at a distance, until they are sure the training wheels can come off without harm.

This is exactly what mentors have done for me in my life. Clyde Harris is a great example of what mentors can do for a person. When I first began working in the insurance inspection and audits industry, I was sent to San Diego to work under Clyde's supervision. My responsibilities included visiting businesses that were insured by our clients and performing fire safety inspections. I would then put together reports with recommendations of ways to make each business safer. Before my reports could finally be submitted, however, Clyde had to review and approve them.

I still have my file of rejected reports, covered with red ink. After three months of working for Clyde and receiving brutal rejections on nearly all of my reports, I was very discouraged. At that moment, a report came back from Clyde with only two words written in red ink: "Nice Report." I had finally passed his test.

Years later, after Ginger and I had begun experiencing success with our own insurance inspection company, we invited Clyde out to Colorado so we could honor him as an important mentor in our business achievements. In recounting our time together in San Diego, he said he really felt bad about being so hard on me, and hoped I wouldn't crack. He admitted that my reports were always good, but that he knew I was capable of doing better.

By pushing me so hard, he forced me to learn, to grow, and to move beyond my limited comfort zone. Clyde challenged me because he cared. He was a mentor who took the time to carefully teach me what he had already learned, and by so doing, he helped give me the tools I needed when it came time to branch out on my own and become an entrepreneur.

Looking back on all the wonderful mentors of my life—Clyde is one of several very meaningful mentors—I strongly believe that those who reach the summits of life only do so with the help of a mentor.

James Ritchie: On Mentors

Like Steve, I am a staunch believer in the importance and power of mentors. In many ways, my life and the successes I've experienced are the products of a large network of mentors, all of whom have in one way or another provided me the examples and lessons I needed to succeed. I want to highlight some of these mentors in order to better illustrate what types of people make good mentors, and the impacts these people make in the lives of those they teach.

I wish everybody could be blessed with a family like mine. Both my parents, Leon and Elda Ritchie, were educated in the University of Hard Knocks and grew up during the Great Depression. Those difficult times toughened them and taught them many of the same lessons written about by people like the Coveys, but my parents understood them long before they were ever formalized in any book or classroom. They learned these principles through long days of hard work, frugal living, and by relying on common sense, logic, and faith.

By the time my brother, Keith, and I came along, my parents were seasoned veterans of both Private and Public Victories, and they worked overtime to make sure both of us understood and bought into the principles they believed were necessary to live a good life.

They worked hard. They were wise with how they used and invested what limited money they had. They went to church and accepted opportunities to serve others. My brother and I trusted them, and because we did, we also trusted these same principles. Looking back, I recognize that growing up on the farm with parents like these was a nearly perfect classroom for learning the habits necessary for success. My childhood served as a platform for eventually moving into the world ready to achieve a Public Victory when I got there.

My family's fires are perhaps the best example of how my parents mentored me. When I was a child, our family's chicken coop, housing over 10,000 pullets (a young female chicken), burned to the ground. These chickens were supposed to spend the next three years laying "golden eggs" for our family. Sometime after this disaster, our hatchery—our farm's primary moneymaker at the time—also burned to the ground during the middle of the night. Neither building was properly insured against fire, and we were left nearly bankrupt.

My dad, who had been fighting this second blaze alongside firefighters and other friends, finally emerged from the smoke and smoldering embers, came into the house where the rest of us were sobbing and feeling mighty sorry for ourselves, and said some words that I have never forgotten: "My hell, aren't we going to have breakfast around here?" He ate, left the house, climbed onto his old tractor, and with the help of many from the community, immediately went to work cleaning the mess and starting over.

For my father, there were no tears of anguish, no "whoa is me" attitude, and no pity parties. He understood that, like all of life, things aren't meant to be easy, and we must learn to take the good along with the bad while continually moving forward. My parents did just that, and our family literally rose from the ashes. Through these difficulties, my parents taught my brother and I how to win the true battles of life.

They don't teach lessons of this caliber at Harvard and Yale.

Along with my parents, my brother has always been an outstanding mentor to me. He learned his chicken farm lessons well. He was elected student body president and graduated high school second in his class before serving a volunteer church mission in Sweden. From there, he graduated with honors from college, finished in the top ten percent of his medical school class, has earned prestigious medical honors, and raised a great family. He continues to serve his country, church, and community with distinction. By living such an exemplary life, Keith provided me both the motivation and the example needed to work hard and live well.

Outside of my immediate family, I was deeply impressed as a young person by several community members, who became mentors to me.

Gordon Mendenhall was a successful and well-known businessman in the Heber Valley of Utah. He was a sharp-dressed, smooth-talking, well-liked personality, and a leader in the community. In my mind, what made Gordon truly successful were his efforts at encouraging others around him. He had a habit of scanning the newspaper and sending short notes of praise and congratulations to any young person mentioned as having done something important or noteworthy. To Gordon, it didn't matter if it was a front-page headline or the last line of the "also mention" section in the back pages. He understood the power of a few positive words, and truly, on those rare occasions when my name somehow made the paper, receiving one of his famous notes raised my self-esteem several notches. I have always remembered this, and have tried to emulate Gordon's example in my adult days.

Along with Gordon, I also looked up to Marion Tree, my high school principal. The lessons he taught me as a youth helped guide me down productive paths, and his advice helped me avoid many dangerous pitfalls. In those times when a mistake had already been made, he taught me how to rectify the situation. I have carried these lessons with me ever since, and they have helped me in my business and entrepreneurial endeavors.

The combined influence of these several childhood mentors really paved the way for me to choose to serve a church mission. It was while serving this mission that I met David B. Haight, the man responsible for teaching me the fundamental principles of The Formula.

If any one of these mentors had not arrived in my life how and when they did, I may never have made it to Scotland. If there had been no mission in Scotland, there would have been no introduction to The Formula, and without the guiding principles of The Formula, my entire life would have run a much different course.

Fortunately, I learned enough from each of these mentors to complete my mission and move on to college, where I met one of the greatest mentors of my entire life, my wife, Carolyn. I've learned much from her example of hard work, as she took full advantage of her education, graduating with distinction from Brigham Young University. Since then, she has worked equally hard as a supportive spouse and life partner, and as an incredible mother of eight children. Carolyn has become a lifelong mentor to our children who, by following her example and teachings, have become successful adults with families of their own.

I could continue telling stories of so many other invaluable mentors in my life—people like Hyrum Smith, Arlen Crouch, John Carmack, Marion D. Hanks, Bernard Brockbanck, Stephen Snow, John Carlile, Sherm Giles, Wayne Thacker, Bob Clyde, Glade Knight, Chris Lansing, McClain Bybee, Dean Christensen, Stan Peterson, and scores of others who have helped me move forward in positive and productive directions—but this would literally fill libraries worth of books.

The point of this exercise, though, is to recognize the many mentors who have made significant impacts in my life. As I reflect on all these people, I realize just how great this impact is.

The truly powerful part about all this is that I believe we could all come up with equally impressive lists of personal mentors who have taught us critical lessons and provided indispensable help. As you continue pursuing your business and life ventures, be mindful of the mentors who cross your path. Recognize what they have to offer, be "quick to observe" what they do, and strive diligently to follow their examples.[28]

The Value Of Strong Mentors

Combining all these ideas, examples, and anecdotes, it's clear that working with a mentor is an irreplaceable component of professional success. Effective mentors will help you navigate the potentially overwhelming world of careers and entrepreneurialism in order to reach your full potential.

By seeking out and adopting good mentors, you fill your life with the people whose support, advice, and real-world, experiential knowledge can lift you above the traps of fear and poor business decisions. They will enable you to take the steps necessary to see your brilliant ideas, lofty goals, and professional aspirations come to life.

Application and Relevance:

1. Understand now that you will never succeed alone; all successes can be traced back to a mentor that helped make the difference.

2. Thoughtfully consider what you're most in need of, and look for influential individuals who can help address these needs. When these types of potential mentors appear, adopt them.

3. Mentoring is a selfless act. The mentor–student relationship should always be positive and uplifting to both parties involved.

4. Show gratitude to your mentors.

5. Mentors will add balance and insight to your vision that will help you succeed.

6. Take a leap of faith, be bold, and start the journey into the unknown by adopting mentors and eventually becoming a mentor to others.

Chapter 06

Financial Fitness

"Financial freedom is a part of the ground happy people stand on."

- James Christiansen

Chapter 6 image - *Discipline is required to become fit, even financially fit.*

Early in our married years, I made some poor decisions that forced Ginger and I into difficult financial situations. Chief among these was my choice to purchase an unnecessary new car.

I had just been promoted and wanted to buy a fancy car to serve as some sort of status symbol. Ginger didn't feel good about this idea, but I felt that driving something nice would communicate to the world my legitimacy as a businessperson and indicate the worth of my recent job advancement. Ginger sensed that there was an important lesson in all this for me to learn, so despite our disagreement, she allowed me to move forward with my decision. I took out a high interest loan and purchased a beautiful Audi 5000.

Quickly after making this purchase, everything fell apart. This one decision drained what little cash we had saved, and before long, we were flat broke. I came to the painful realization that I had made a huge mistake, and all because of personal pride. In the end Ginger was right, this really was an important lesson I needed to learn.

I tried to return the car to the bank. They didn't want it, but finally agreed to take it for a discount. This meant I still owed money on it, but at least the source of the headache was gone. Because of this whole ordeal, we couldn't afford rent. We were too embarrassed to ask our parents for help, and thankfully, our church congregation was able to use some church welfare funds to help us that month. From that day on, I vowed that I would never again put my family or myself in such a predicament.

It was a short time later that we met the Ritchies, and began learning from them the principles of Financial Fitness. This proved to be one of the most important things James taught us. As Ginger and I have incorporated this concept into our lives, we've successfully avoided any repeat Audi debacles, and have experienced great results. Understanding how to effectively manage our financial resources has been a critical component to all our successes. In the following section, James Ritchie outlines and explains the concept of Financial Fitness.

James Ritchie: Financial Fitness

For some people, wealth is a measuring stick of status. This type of attitude often leads people to focus too much on money. For these individuals, wealth creates pride and arrogance, and thus destroys their potential for doing good in the world.

For others, however, wealth is a tool of service and sharing. For them, success is measured by the amount of "goods and services" that can be given to those less fortunate and in need. This attitude maintains a broader perspective in which money is not an end in itself, but is recognized as only a single piece in the larger puzzle that is life.

I believe the latter perspective to be the most meaningful and productive. Self-reliance is the true goal, not being rich. Working to provide resources sufficient to meet our needs—along with a little extra—opens doors of opportunity. When we view money as the means of becoming self-reliant rather than an end in itself, we are more likely to avoid becoming prideful, arrogant, and self-centered. Maintaining a healthy attitude toward money also makes it easier to recognize and take advantage of opportunities to serve others; and in the end, this is the true joy of financial independence.

When Carolyn and I began our married life, we had little in terms of financial means. But we were blessed with great backgrounds that had taught us the value of hard work. After adding some university training and The Formula to this basic understanding, we were set to venture out on our own and begin making our marks on the world.

Very early in my entrepreneurial efforts, I discovered *The Richest Man in Babylon*, by George Clason. Reading this book, and following what I'd learned from it, saved me from many dead ends and unproductive detours. It was the most powerful read of my young life.

The chart below outlines some of the key concepts I learned from Clason's book, and summarizes the principle of Financial Fitness. By following this outline, Carolyn and I have been able to avoid the temptation to surround ourselves with material things, and have learned instead to focus on accumulating the appreciating assets that allowed us to retire in our mid-30s. Without the guiding principles of Financial Fitness, we may never have achieved the type of financial independence necessary to fully commit ourselves to a life of service.

Financial Fitness

$ Work

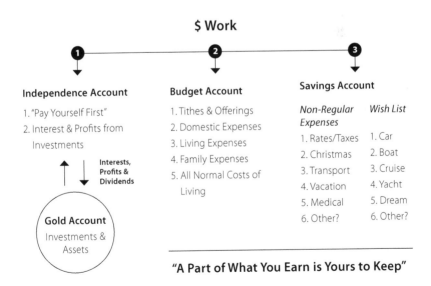

Independence Account

1. "Pay Yourself First"
2. Interest & Profits from Investments

Interests, Profits & Dividends

Gold Account
Investments & Assets

Budget Account

1. Tithes & Offerings
2. Domestic Expenses
3. Living Expenses
4. Family Expenses
5. All Normal Costs of Living

Savings Account

Non-Regular Expenses	*Wish List*
1. Rates/Taxes	1. Car
2. Christmas	2. Boat
3. Transport	3. Cruise
4. Vacation	4. Yacht
5. Medical	5. Dream
6. Other?	6. Other?

"A Part of What You Earn is Yours to Keep"

The first and most important principle of Financial Fitness is hard work. Throughout my life, my parents, The Formula, and Clason's book all reiterated this as the foundation of any business and entrepreneurial success. The Bible also adds credibility to this principle when, in the book of Genesis, God tells Adam and Eve they are to earn their keep "in the sweat of thy face."[29] Without sustained and consistent hard work, nothing else is possible.

The second principle of Financial Fitness comes from Arkad, the hero of Clason's book, when he says, "Pay yourself first."[30] This concept directs us to use our income to pay ourselves a portion of everything we earn—Clason's text suggests at least 10%—rather than using our income to buy material "stuff." This money comprises the Independence Account. The power of this concept is that it overturns the common belief of our capitalistic world that we should not only work for our needs, but for all of our "wants" as well, and then save anything else that's left over. This prevailing philosophy is flawed, however, because after spending money on all the material stuff that sounds appealing, there's seldom anything left for anything else. Paying yourself first shifts the focus away from consuming and places it on saving and growing a sizable base of funds.

The third principle of Financial Fitness also comes from Arkad, who teaches, "A part of all you earn is yours to keep."[31] This concept provides a more refined definition regarding what exactly should be done with the money we pay ourselves first. These funds should be set aside as cash, and then should be allowed to accumulate until we have enough to begin investing in appreciating assets or other business opportunities—this is the Gold Account. At this point, any profits, dividends, or interest should be put back into the original Independence Account, and as this account continues to grow larger, continue using it to make increasingly lucrative investments.

This cycle goes around and around until the accumulated asset base generated through profits, dividends, interest, or capital gains is sufficient to provide an annual income that will take care of all living expenses. At this point you have become financially independent and self-reliant.

Paying ourselves first not only provides the funds needed to begin investing and working toward financial independence and self-reliance, it also forces us to be more frugal with the other two accounts included in the diagram: the Budget Account and the Savings Account.

The Budget Account must be cranked down to the bare minimum in order to allow more money to go into the Independence Account. The Budget Account should usually be something like a checkbook that receives barely enough to cover the frugal written budget from paycheck to paycheck. It should go from "rich" to "zero" through the course of each budget cycle.

The third account is the Savings Account, and it's devoted to covering any irregular expenses such as holidays, birthdays, insurance, and emergencies. This is the account that also covers any "wish list" items—a new truck, a yacht, a jet—those non-appreciating assets that are mostly for fun or as a personal indulgence. While it's crucial to never allow the consumption of material objects to become the main focus of your business and financial endeavors, there's nothing wrong with making a "wish list" and rewarding yourself once in a while for your hard work. Just be sure this never takes higher priority than the Budget Account or Independence Account.

Now take some time to visualize in your mind this beautiful financial plan. Visualize the way that paying yourself first and keeping it will result in a growing pile of appreciating assets and/or business assets. Consider the way that frugal living will work together with compounding interest and asset accumulation to propel you ever closer to financial independence and self-reliance.

As you work hard to grow your Independence Account to the point that it reaches your financial goals, you will experience not only great joy but inner peace as well, knowing you are in control of your life and are working to maximize your opportunities. Self-worth, self-esteem, and productivity will all expand, and as they do, your opportunities to do good in the world and serve others will also become greater. Thus, your self-reliance will ultimately bring you to the true purpose of life and the source of greatest happiness: giving back and building a better world.

Application and Relevance:

1. Financial independence isn't being rich, it's being self-reliant. And self-reliance is defined as having sufficient for your needs plus a little extra.

2. Don't view financial independence as an end in itself, but as a stepping-stone toward the greater goals of inner peace and serving others.

3. The keys to growing your Independence Account is to pay yourself first and to keep a part of everything you earn in the form of investable cash. This will provide a base with which to begin investing and funding business ventures.

4. Write out a frugal monthly budget and stick to it.

5. Maintain a Savings Account to cover any irregular expenses and "wish list" items.

6. Remember that giving back instead of accumulating more generates the purest joys in life.

Chapter 07

The Personal Constitution [32]

"Vision without effort is daydreaming; effort without vision is drudgery; but vision, coupled with effort, will obtain the prize."

- Thomas S. Monson,
President of the Church of Jesus Christ of Latter-Day Saints[33]

Chapter 7 image - *When charting our course, true principles become a compass and our confidence.*

Ginger and I didn't discover the concept of a Personal Constitution until we were in our 50s. We immediately found it fascinating. As soon as we learned about it, we both began working to create our own Personal Constitutions. We prayed to have a clearer picture of the people we wanted to become, and began attempting to formalize these desires through writing them down into personal, life-guiding documents.

Putting together my Personal Constitution took over four months of writing, pondering, praying, and re-writing. I've since learned that my Personal Constitution is most meaningful when I allow it to become dynamic, capable of growing and evolving according to the changes of life. So I continue to work on it, alter it, and expand it.

Throughout the entire process of writing a Personal Constitution, I've discovered new and important things about myself, and continue to do so as I allow this document to guide my life. My Personal Constitution is a document I consider deeply personal and highly inspired. This is a concept I wish I had discovered in my twenties; but the point is, it's never too late to begin developing one.

James Ritchie: On Personal Constitutions

Introduction

If a modern day Moses were invited by God to the top of Mt. Sinai to receive Phase II of the Ten Commandments, I speculate that the stone tablet engraved by the finger of God resulting from this interaction would contain something like the "productivity pyramid" pictured below:[34]

I also speculate that the motivation behind such a meeting would be concern on God's part for humanity's inability to live the commandments and guidelines already provided in scripture, which are ultimately aimed at helping us become "perfect, even as [our] Father in Heaven is perfect."[35]

After watching mankind's pathetic, and typically feeble, attempts to follow these commandments, God would invite Moses back to the mountain to receive a second set of tablets. These new teachings would provide concrete steps enabling individuals to consistently live the principles required for success, and more importantly, to actually become individuals of success.

I recognize the hyperbolic nature of this analogy, and I also recognize the heavy emphasis I've placed on biblical ideas regarding God. The real point of all this, though, is to stress the importance of the seemingly simple principles of the above productivity pyramid. My analogy is also intended to highlight the need for each of us to have role models who inspire us to become better. Whether your idea of an exemplary figure is Jesus Christ, a successful local entrepreneur, or a world renowned professional, you need to have some person in your life who you look up to, and who inspires you to become better.

Becoming better—a better entrepreneur, family member, friend, associate, and all-around human being—is what the Personal Constitution is all about. A Personal Constitution is a single document outlining who you want to be and what you're going to do to accomplish this objective. The Personal Constitution becomes the guiding document for how you live your daily life, and when followed, will allow you to attain your loftiest goals and desires. In crafting your Personal Constitution, the productivity pyramid serves as a basic outline, directing attention to the most critical aspects of goal setting and goal achieving.

Governing Values

Without a firm and immovable foundation, the pyramids of ancient Egypt would have crumbled thousands of years ago. But today, thanks to their large and sturdy foundations, they continue to stand as strong as ever.

Our lives are the same. We need a foundational system of values upon which to build. When we are without a set of values, our lives tend to wander aimlessly, and even if we don't completely crash and burn, we certainly won't reach our full potential without some sort of foundation to give us constant strength and guidance.

The first step in writing a Personal Constitution, therefore, is to identify those values or personal qualities most important to you. These are the attributes you most admire in your role models. These are the qualities that define what type of person you ultimately want yourself to become—don't consider yourself as you are now, but as you'd like to someday become. Some common defining values that may appear on peoples' lists include integrity, ethical living, loyalty, morality, friendliness, being charitable, and being trustworthy. Whatever your list of values includes, these ideas become the foundation of your entire Personal Constitution.

After you've brainstormed a list of values, it's time to prioritize them. Rank them in order from the single most important value to those that are less important to you. This is a critical exercise and should be taken seriously, because the way you prioritize your values has serious consequences when it comes time to implement your Personal Constitution into your everyday life.

To illustrate the importance of prioritizing values, let's suppose that a person's list includes the following two ideas: financial independence and honesty. If being financially independent is of a higher priority than being honest, how do you think this person will act when a business opportunity comes along in which a failure to disclose important information could allow him or her to pocket some extra cash? Consider, on the other hand, what this person might do in the same situation if he or she had placed being honest at a higher priority than financial independence.

The way we prioritize the values and personal qualities that are most important to us dictates our actions. This is why it's important to seriously consider what type of person you eventually want to become and think about what types of personal values will get you there.

Keep in mind the principles of The Formula when trying to prioritize what's truly most important. When you do this, it will be clear that focusing on those qualities and values that will allow you to become a charitable and service-oriented individual are more important than solely focusing on financial concerns. In fact, making service the ultimate focus of all you do will actually make you a more successful businessperson, professional, and entrepreneur.

Once you've prioritized your list of personal values and qualities, it's time to begin writing your Personal Constitution. Begin with your number one, most important personal value and write a sentence that begins "I am," and ends with a description of that value. Obviously, you won't yet be the type of person this statement describes, but using the "I am" structure provides a positive and direct language that will direct you toward action rather than mere abstract thinking or wishing.

As an example, a Christian may write this type of a sentence: "I am like the Savior."

Then build this first sentence into a paragraph by defining what exactly this means to you. Continuing our example: "I am like the Savior. I think the way He thought, act the way He acted, speak the way He spoke, and treat everyone the way He treated them."

Another example of a common paragraph that may be found on many Personal Constitutions reads:

"I am totally honest in all my personal, family, and business dealings. I am trusted by my fellow beings and would do nothing to damage or harm any of those relationships."

Yet another reads:

"I am financially self-reliant. I take care of my financial 'wants' and 'needs' from earnings, profits, dividends, interest, and other means of return from my businesses and investments. I earn all this without needing to go to 'work' everyday."

To identify your values, picture your ideal self—don't only consider what you want to be, but really ponder who you want to be. Look to inspirational role models in helping construct this image. From there, make a list of all the attributes and qualities that make up your ideal future self. Prioritize these values and qualities by order of importance. Begin drafting your Personal Constitution through writing "I am" sentences and expanding them into more detailed paragraphs.

Long Term Goals

After you have a written and prioritized set of values, it's time to move up the pyramid and focus on setting goals. When you set goals, you identify what needs to be done to transform yourself from the person you are now into the ideal self you've started visualizing.

When setting goals, it's most effective to break them into long term and short term goals. For the purposes of writing a Personal Constitution, we'll consider long term goals those goals that embody your ideal self. In setting long term goals, you should build directly off the "I am" statements of your identifying values exercise.

All goals must be written out in "I will" statements. Such language is direct and binding; it commits you to take action and complete tasks.

An example of a properly written long term goal might read:

"I will be financially independent by the age of 55, meaning that I will be able to live off the profits, interest, or dividends of my businesses and investments without the need to 'go to work.'" (As a side note, nearly everyone I know who has reached this wonderful state of financial independence still "goes to work" but the great part is that such individuals don't have to do it for financial survival. Instead, they do it because they love it!)

Long term goals begin mapping out the concrete objectives that must be accomplished in order to become the person you aspire to become.

Short Term Goals

After setting long term goals, it's time to focus on setting short term goals—those things you will do during the current year that will move you closer to accomplishing your long term goals.

A short term goal could read like this:

"I will add to my Independence Account 13% of my gross earnings and 75% of any capital gains or profits I generate this year."

Once again, this goal uses clear and direct language—language that commits to action. It is clear and attainable, and because it's measurable, there's an objective way to determine whether or not success is achieved.

The Daily Task List

The apex of our productivity pyramid is the daily task list. This is, in my opinion, the most fun and the most productive piece of the Personal Constitution.

After getting seven hours of sleep at night, you're left with 17 remaining hours, or 1,020 minutes in the day. I call these minutes Productivity Points, and you have 1,020 of them every single day for the rest of your life. Coincidentally, that's the exact same number every other human being on the planet—and every one of your competitors—also receives as a free gift every morning. The only way to get the most out of each day is to focus on taking full advantage of every Productivity Point. Your daily task list ensures that this happens.[36]

Your daily task list should be a written out list of tasks and personal assignments that you will accomplish that day. When making these daily lists, always consider whether or not each item on the list will move you closer to achieving your short term goals.

Write your daily task list using sentences beginning with the phrase: "Today I will." The consistent use of this type of language throughout all levels of goal setting and planning maintains focus on direct and consistent action.

Daily task lists are so powerful because they provide the guidance needed each and every day. They become the motor for your progression. The only way to travel the long road between where you're at today and where you need to be to achieve all your long term goals can be a daunting one, and it can only be traveled through short and consistent daily steps. By making effective daily task lists, you maximize your daily allotment of Productivity Points. As you do this, you'll begin feeling the power of controlling your life. You'll witness your personal productivity increase each day, and your feelings of self-confidence and self-worth will climb into the stratosphere.

The End Result

Now for the punch line: When the way you use your 1,020 daily Productivity Points is driven by your bottom line—your governing values and the goals they necessitate—you will not only see a marked increase in your personal productivity, but you will also begin to approach an unparalleled state of inner peace.

When you prioritize your values appropriately, you will naturally set the type of short and long term goals that will help you become a better, more loving, more serving, and more content individual. When you're serious about achieving these goals, you'll begin planning each day, and as you follow these plans, you'll find yourself taking full advantage of every Productivity Point—every minute—you've been given.

The fulfillment of your daily task lists will lead to the accomplishment of your short term goals. Reaching short term goals is progress toward achieving your long term goals. And as you gradually reach these goals, you will one day become the type of human being you've always wanted to become.

Along the way, you will witness yourself becoming financially self-reliant. You will experience the positive feelings of living an honest life. You will notice yourself becoming a better husband, wife, sibling, or friend. You will spend more time working to build up others than you do yourself. You will increase in Christ-like characteristics such as love, charity, kindness, and commitment. Your resolve to live a daily life devoted to doing good and being productive will strengthen.

As you undergo each of these "growth spurts," you will feel better about yourself and your life; you will become ever more peaceful and happy.

The key is to make the most of your precious minutes today by keeping in mind what you want to become tomorrow. Let this vision drive the goals you set, the plans you make, and the actions you take. As you begin living this way, you'll discover what a loving Heavenly Father had in mind when He sent us down to experience life. You will begin experiencing the inner peace of striving for perfection, and although true perfection is ultimately unattainable in this life, such is the path eventually leading to eternal joy.

Create Your Own Personal Constitution: Steve's How-To Guide

As a conclusion to the ideas outlined by James, let me offer a step-by-step guide for writing a Personal Constitution. This guide will help you actually sit down and begin drafting this life-changing document.

- To begin building your own Personal Constitution, find some time when you can be alone in a place of peaceful quiet. Think about the person you currently are. Next, take time to ponder the type of person you want to become in the future. If you're honest with yourself, there will always be a chasm between the two, but that's okay, the point of this exercise is to help you identify what you truly value, what your deepest desires are, and where your greatest hopes lie. This is how you begin developing your foundation of governing values.

- Once you've taken the time to meditate and ponder, begin writing short phrases or words describing what you want to become.

An example from my Personal Constitution is the phrase "graciousness and caring."

- Next, review your phrases or words and determine how to incorporate them into a goal statement and personal affirmation. It usually helps to ask yourself why you included each item in your initial list.

The example from my Personal Constitution now looks like this: "I believe that every person deserves to be treated as a child of God, and that the quality of graciousness allows those I interact with to feel the love of God through me. I will endeavor to stop thinking about myself all the time, and will instead focus on the well being of others. By so doing, the cares of the world will evaporate and the cares of God's children will be better met through me. I am gracious and caring."

Note that my statement closes with an affirmative statement. It's important to imbed these positive thoughts into your subconscious because we really do become that which we most think about.

- Continue expanding each item from your initial brainstorm into these types of statements. Remember, though, that there's no perfect way to write a Personal Constitution. Follow the inspiration of your inner voice, and feel free to adjust this process if needed.

- After you've expanded each of your ideas, leave them alone and ponder them for a couple weeks. They may change, and you might tweak them. If so, that's great, always remember that your Personal Constitution is dynamic.

- After you feel good about the expanded statements you've written, prioritize them in order of importance.

  For example, my statement regarding graciousness and caring ranks fifth on my list.

- At this point, leave your written work alone for at least another week. At the close of the week, revisit and refine your ideas. This prioritized list of detailed statements—including definitions of values, goals, and affirmations—is now your working Personal Constitution. Consult it frequently, and don't be afraid to make adjustments as you progress through life.

- Now that you have a working Personal Constitution, make a couple hardcopies of the document. Keep one for yourself and consider giving another copy to your spouse, life partner, or another trustworthy confidant. By sharing this with someone you trust, you build into the Personal Constitution a sense of accountability—there is now another person who knows your goals and who can help hold you responsible for how well you do or do not progress toward reaching them.

- With your written Personal Constitution in hand, you're now ready to follow James' advice in setting long and short term goals and making daily task lists.

- Finally, as you start living life according to your Personal Constitution, don't be discouraged if who you are today isn't yet the person you truly desire to become. Your Personal Constitution should make you stretch. It should make you focus and work. Striving to become is often more important than actually becoming, the journey more important than the destination. As you follow your Personal Constitution, the roads you walk will be rewarding, and in the end, you will find yourself equipped with all the tools needed to finally make your goals a reality.

Application and Relevance:

1. A Personal Constitution is a document to guide your life. It provides a way to think about the type of person you'd like to become and then map out how you'll become that person.

2. The foundation of an effective Personal Constitution is identifying your governing values. Look to role models and inspirational figures to help you prioritize what attributes and personal qualities will allow you to become the best person you can possibly become.

3. Use your governing values to help set long and short term goals.

4. Begin achieving these goals be writing and executing daily task lists. Focus on maximizing your daily allotment of Productivity Points.

5. Record and consult your Personal Constitution regularly to stay on track. Give a copy to someone you trust to increase accountability.

6. Always remember: If you stay the course—long term, short term, and today—you will eventually become the product of your dreams and aspirations.

Chapter 08

Giving Back

"I knew a man, they thought him mad, the more he gave, the more he had."

- Anonymous

Chapter 8 image - *As we travel through uncharted territory, we leave signs to those who follow, showing them the wisest path ahead.*

Our Epiphany

One morning, while on a spring break vacation with my family in southern California, I sat watching the ocean and feeling the breeze on my face. In my personal readings, I had just finished *The Go-Giver* by Bob Burg and John David Mann.[37] This book suggests that using business as a means of giving back and helping others leads to unexpected benefits in the life of the giver. As I pondered this message and enjoyed the beauty of the world around me, I was overcome with a sense of gratitude for the experience of being. This gratitude gave me a strong desire to increase the ways in which I gave back to those around me.

For Ginger and I, giving back had always been a principle of central importance in our personal lives. As members of the LDS church, we pay "tithing"—we pay ten percent of all our income to the church as a donation. This money helps pay various costs such as building new church buildings and contributing to the church's global humanitarian efforts. On top of this, we also make monthly donations to our local congregation. This money stays in the community to help those in need.

Despite the importance of giving in our personal lives, it was still not something we focused on in our business lives. Remember the chapter on duplicity? We realized that we needed to bridge the gap between these two important aspects of our lives, and come up with some strategy that would allow our efforts at US–Reports to become as focused on giving back as we were striving to be in our own personal lives.

At this same time, and seemingly by chance, my friend Mark introduced me to an associate who, it just so happened, assisted in helping companies and other organizations develop charity models. This new acquaintance helped us formulate, organize, and implement a system through which US–Reports could regularly donate a portion of its earnings to charitable causes.

We quickly set up charitable donor advisory funds with Deseret Trust Company, and they handled the legal and logistical aspects of ensuring that donated funds were successfully delivered to the appropriate charity. With this in place, Ginger and I decided to commit a certain percentage of our total revenues (not profits) to our clients' charities of choice. The more clients used our services, the more revenue they paid us, and the more they would be able to donate to their own good causes.

This type of system was new to Ginger and I; we had never done anything like this in our professional and entrepreneurial activities. In our industry, we operate on small profit margins, and suddenly setting aside a chunk of revenues for our new donations program was initially scary. Something like this had never been in the company's budget, and we weren't sure how it would work out.

Despite our apprehensions, we went ahead with plans. I knew that the combination of reading *The Go-Giver*, feeling a strong desire to use business as a means of giving back, unexpectedly meeting a professional who helped strategize charitable donations programs, and having a board of directors that unanimously supported such a program was not a coincidence. I recognized this as yet another instance of divinely inspired and organized guidance. This assurance ultimately gave Ginger and I the courage to move past our initial fears and fully implement our new donations program.

In its first year, the program had 120 participants and distributed over a quarter of a million dollars to charities close to our clients' hearts. Additionally, US–Reports made its own donations to charities that Ginger and I had chosen.

The first year we began this program was also the first really devastating year of the economic downturn. Amazingly, US–Reports had a very good year. In fact, our company became more profitable after we established a formulated initiative for giving back. Our company has continued to focus on giving back, and as this has become an increasingly significant aspect of the company's culture, we have witnessed continued financial success and stability regardless of the economic turmoil around us.

While I firmly believe that US–Reports' financial security has been a blessing directly resulting from our efforts to give back, it's important to understand that we should never give or serve with the expectation that our lives will suddenly become more prosperous as a result of our service. Giving back must be sincere and selfless, not superficial and self-serving.

Giving back is important, not because of the potential blessings it may provide, but because of the way it changes hearts. The key to this change is alignment. When we serve others and give to those in need, we become instruments in the hands of God. We join Him in His work of blessing peoples' lives. As we continue to serve and give back, we demonstrate to God that we are individuals whom He can trust to do His will and to carry out His work of love and service. Through service, we align our hearts, desires, and actions with God's will, and ultimately, our acts of giving become conduits through which God's blessings flow.

When an entire organization or business works together to serve and give back, the collective nearness to God such service facilitates has profound effects on the organization as a whole. As US–Reports began focusing on its charitable giving, Ginger and I noticed a distinct change in everyone involved with the company. Everything we or any of our employees did became more purposeful. Suddenly, every worker at US–Reports more fully appreciated his or her role in controlling costs and improving efficiencies, because the better the company operated, the more lives were blessed. This dynamic is powerful—it puts more meaning into the workplace.

While the financial blessings the company received were truly remarkable, the change in our company's culture was more powerful and more meaningful than anything else. An associate of mine named Richard Ball accurately characterizes giving back as the means through which our lives become vibrant and colorful.[38] Serving others is truly what gives life meaning and purpose.

Ideally, your entrepreneurial ventures will be such that they inherently change the world for the better, but always keep in mind that nothing changes the world more powerfully than the act of giving with a heart that's aligned with God. As you use your professional activities as a means of giving back, recognize the blessings involved: the blessings you help bring about in the lives of those you serve, the blessings you may receive, and especially your personal nearness to God.

Make It Happen

Through our experiences, we have learned that there are some important guidelines necessary for any company to follow in order to establish a framework for giving back:

1. **Bridge The Gap:** The only way to create a company dedicated to giving back and helping those in need is to ensure that your personal life and your professional life are consistent with one another. Congruency between all facets of life is a theme throughout this entire book, and the only way to make giving back an important enough priority to become meaningful on a company-wide level is to make it a high priority in your personal

life as well.

If giving back and serving had not already been important principles in which we believed, Ginger and I may not have had the faith to implement an official company policy of giving back.

When you maintain the same priorities and value systems in all settings and aspects of your life, you will have the conviction needed to act consistently and confidently. This type of firm dedication is critical when working to establish a plan for giving back in your entrepreneurial endeavors.

2. **Plan On Giving:** Because Ginger and I have always planned on immediately donating ten percent of our income as tithing to our church, it's never really felt like a hardship. When we construct a fixed plan for taking a specific course of action, we eliminate any room for doubt or second-guessing ourselves. When we make plans, we make a decision so that when it comes time to act, we already know what we will do. Planning paves the way for accomplishment.

This becomes especially important when trying to implement a strategy for giving back into your entrepreneurial and professional activities. Working with professional consultants and third-party charitable trust companies can be incredibly helpful. But whatever your method, the key is to make giving a planned activity. Make it an official policy and establish a fixed program through which funds will regularly and safely be donated to meaningful charitable causes. When you plan on giving, you make it a part of your company's daily operations, and it will become a fundamental principle in your company's culture of success.

3. **Focus On Stewardship:** When putting together your strategy for giving back, it's important to consider the principle of stewardship. In life, we all have certain responsibilities and commitments we must fulfill. One of the most basic of these responsibilities is caring and providing for ourselves and our families—this is ultimately why we work and why we strive to make a good living.

   Remember that a good steward doesn't squander his or her resources. Giving to others at the expense of your own family is inappropriate because it ignores a basic responsibility of all human beings. As you consider how to allocate revenues toward charitable causes, be sure you don't become a bad steward by neglecting any of your duties.

   Carefully consider what you and your own family realistically need. Along with the regular living expenses of housing, food, healthcare, clothes, and education, be sure you have enough for savings and for occasional fun family activities. If you have employees, be sure they're appropriately paid and generously provided for.

   After ensuring that all responsibilities and duties have been fully met, you can devote your remaining resources to giving back. If you effectively manage your funds, you should always be able to find a way to give back and serve others while also providing for the needs of yourself, your family, and your employees. Finding such a balance is good entrepreneurial stewardship.

4. **Consider Money, Time, And Sweat:** As you think about ways you and your company can give back and help others, remember

that money isn't the only way to serve. While donating funds is always needed, donating your time and personal effort are also extremely helpful and deeply rewarding. Strive to become intimately familiar with the work of charity by personally visiting the homeless, serving in soup kitchens, and visiting with leaders of local charities.

After establishing its first giving back initiative, our company expanded its charitable efforts to the point that teams of employees and associates donated time and labor every month to such programs as food kitchens, fundraising carwashes, and Habitat for Humanity.

Believe me, when you stand in a serving line feeding the homeless, you suddenly realize that your own challenges really aren't so bad. The act of giving, and the subsequent experience of seeing some degree of light and hope come into the lives of those you serve is worth every dollar spent, minute of time donated, and drop of sweat given.

5. **Track Progress:** After constructing a model of giving and implementing it as a part of your company's everyday culture and operations, it's important to track the progress and the outcome of your efforts.

After beginning our company's giving back program, Ginger and I began keeping a philanthropy journal. We use this journal to record any touching stories we hear or any expressions of gratitude we receive from those our company has helped. We don't do this to build up a portfolio of great things we've done, but simply to record gratitude: theirs and ours. This journal helps us realize how much we have to be grateful for, and reinforces our efforts to serve others by highlighting the impact such efforts can make.

As we've tracked the progress of our company's efforts to give back, we've witnessed the way that service becomes deeply cooperative. Suddenly, Ginger, myself, our employees, our clients, our contacts at Deseret Trust Company, volunteers at specific charitable organizations, and local activists are all working together on the same team in an effort to bless the lives of others—oftentimes people we'll never even meet. As our company becomes one of many threads in a larger tapestry of service, Ginger and I have repeatedly felt humbled and awed to be part of a global and collaborative effort to change this world for the better.

Wrapping It Up

From my own experiences, I've learned that when we focus our professional efforts on giving back and helping others, our souls are enlivened, we become more closely knit to work associates, clients, and employees, and we ourselves become more humble.

One of the greatest teachings ever recorded on giving back is found in scripture: "And now, if God, who has created you, on whom you are dependent for your lives and for all that ye have and are, doth grant unto you whatsoever ye ask that is right, in faith, believing that ye shall receive, O then, how ye ought to impart of the substance that ye have one to another."[39]

As this passage teaches, the better we understand the central role God plays in our entrepreneurial and professional successes, the better we understand the importance of giving back. Indeed, anything we receive in this life isn't fully ours to begin with—it's been given to us through the blessings and kindness of our loving Heavenly Father. Knowing this, how can we feel justified in not sharing, serving, and giving back?

Yet (and this is the truly incredible part), in what seems to be a paradox, the more we devote our resources and efforts toward helping those around us, the more God blesses us with happiness and safety. As Jesus taught in the New Testament: "Give, and it shall be given unto you; good measure . . . and running over, shall men give into your bosom. For with the same measure that ye mete withal it shall be measured unto you again."[40]

Application and Relevance:

1. Giving back isn't for social status—it's to help those in need.

2. The process of giving back on a regular and formulated basis will strengthen your businesses and the lives within them in the following ways:

   a. Giving back lends purpose to your actions and success.

   b. The act of giving will add color and vibrancy to your life.

   c. Giving back and serving others aligns your heart with the will of God, and helps you draw closer to Him.

3. It's critical to develop a formulation for giving back each month. In doing so, remember to:

   a. Bridge The Gap

   b. Plan On Giving

   c. Focus On Stewardship

   d. Consider Money, Time, And Sweat

   e. Track Progress

4. Always have an attitude of giving, even if you can't presently give as much as you would like.

Chapter 09

The Unseen Difference

"I have never thought of writing for reputation and honor. What I have in my heart must come out; that is the reason why I compose."

- Ludwig van Beethoven

Chapter 9 image - *Experiences shared and lessons learned in the quiet moments of life are often the most meaningful.*

It's All About Others

During the time Ginger and I lived in southern California, there was a man in our local church congregation who really intrigued me. He was one of the friendliest and all around nicest people I'd ever met. Whenever I saw him he was dressed like a gas station worker, his hard-toed, low-top black shoes completing the look. He and his wife were happy and content, and with their wonderful family of 12 children taking up an entire pew at church, they looked like the Clampetts from *The Beverly Hillbillies*. He and I soon got to know each other as we worked together in several church service responsibilities, and we quickly became close friends.

Ginger and I had never visited my friend and his family at their home until one day, when he invited us to his house to eat snacks and socialize. We were shocked when we arrived at his 8,000 square foot mansion. It turns out that my friend owned several gas stations, was involved with various other investment and real estate projects, and was very successfully involved in the stock market.

The way this man interacted with others was as humble and unselfish as was his physical appearance, neither of which fit the stereotype of the self-centered and greedy millionaire. He never told stories about himself, but rather, would focus on building up those around him. When asked about his business activities, he was very open and honest, but never arrogant. It was clear that his goal was not to flaunt his success in a self-aggrandizing manner, but to be a positive influence in the lives of others.

My friend didn't know it at the time, but he quickly became an adopted mentor of mine. The lesson he taught me has proven to be a powerful secret for achieving success in any life endeavor, business included. While the world is full of me, me, and more me, my friend taught that the greatest success comes when you understand how much life is not about "me." The most meaningful success comes from focusing outwards, on others. My friend taught me this through the way he lived, treated others, and handled his business successes.

Sadly, the world is full of professional athletes, entertainment superstars, and wealthy businesspeople who take all the credit for their own achievements. They are concerned only with their own success and their own recognition, and all too often, these self-serving attitudes are rewarded by the praise of an idol-worshipping public.

People like my friend stand in stark (and relieving) contrast to these types of people. If you've ever spent time with a multi-millionaire who couldn't care less whether or not anybody knows it, you know how thrilling it is to be with such a person. Interacting with these types of superstars is much more rewarding and powerful than spending time with a superstar whose only concern is him or herself.

While I certainly benefited greatly from my friendship and interactions with this man, I believe that he also benefited from choosing to live such a serving, unselfish lifestyle. Scripture teaches us an important principle regarding service to others: "And behold, I tell you these things that ye may learn wisdom; that ye may learn that when ye are in the service of your fellow beings ye are only in the service of your God."[41]

In the New Testament, Jesus shares a similar insight: "For whosoever will save his life shall lose it: and whosoever will lose his life for my sake shall find it. For what is a man profited, if he shall gain the whole world, and lose his own soul?"[42]

As revealed in these passages, when we focus on serving others and uplifting those around us, we ourselves are blessed. These blessings appear in our present lives and, more importantly, help prepare us for the blessings of eternity. By serving others, we demonstrate our love for and faith in God. The closer we align ourselves with God, the more He can bless us in all our life endeavors.

I firmly believe that my friend received divine guidance and aid in his business pursuits because he had demonstrated his desires to use personal success to help and inspire those around him.

Success Is Not A Solo Project

Along with teaching the importance of serving others, and highlighting the blessings that come from a service-oriented lifestyle, the scriptures also emphasize how deeply dependent we are on God.

After being reminded that we were made from dust and we will all someday return to dust, who can feel justified in taking full credit for any successes experienced in life?[43] Don't we all depend on Deity for every breath we take? Recognizing that our survival from one day to the next—indeed, our very being—is ultimately dependent on someone outside ourselves is an important truth to understand.

When we consider this principle of truth within the more specific context of professional success, it becomes very apparent that such achievements are also not ours alone. Success in the business world is always the product of numerous contributors. Partners, mentors, associates, and clients are all critical components in the success of any individual businessperson.

When we combine an understanding of the collaborative nature of professional success with the recognition that business and financial successes are ultimately intended to bless the lives of others, it becomes possible to become the unseen difference.

Be The Unseen Difference

The unseen difference is guidance, mentorship, and leadership given and shared "behind the scenes." It's a certain way of passing along lessons we've learned and insights we've been fortunate enough to discover.

The manner in which these things are shared is important. Nobody wants to learn from a bombastic personality. Even if such people have valuable insights to share, the essence of any message they deliver is lost because of their conceit.

The unseen difference embodies one of the most personal, genuine, and in the end, successful ways to share and receive wisdom. When acting as the unseen difference, a person regards his or her knowledge and experience as sacred, and shares these things in humility and love. These lessons are almost always the most powerful. They are most often shared in the quiet settings of a home or a porch; seldom are they communicated from a podium.

In a great book about the importance of relationships, Tom Rath outlines eight roles to be filled by people in a relationship:[44]

- Builder
- Champion
- Collaborator
- Companion
- Connector
- Energizer
- Mind opener
- Navigator

He then urges readers to discover which of these roles they perform within their relationships with friends and associates. While I'm not going to take the time to fully explore these eight characteristics, I do want to focus on Rath's main point of encouraging us to consider what unique contributions we can make in our relationships with others.

Perhaps none of Rath's relationship roles fully applies to you, but the important thing is to find your special niche in the contributions you can make, and then focus on using this to become a positive force in the lives of those around you.

I've discovered my natural tendency is to be more of a connector, as I love connecting folks with other people or ideas I believe will assist them in achieving their dreams. One of my favorite things to do is to give copies of great books to people trying to make a difference in the world. Anytime I read a book that makes a particularly strong impact in my life, I buy 10 copies of it, keep these copies on my bookshelf, and give them away whenever I feel so prompted. Over the years, I've shared books with restaurant owners, hotel operators, insurance professionals, bankers, real estate moguls, and many other people.

In his book *Silos Politics and Turf Wars*, Patrick Lencioni talks about folks who construct "silos" in which to hoard information.[45] Such silos kill creativity and build walls of distrust between the hoarder of information and the rest of the world. Hoarding knowledge and wisdom accomplishes nothing productive. The hoarder's scope of potentially positive impacts to be made is severely hampered, and because no sharing or collaboration is taking place, nobody else benefits from whatever knowledge has been hoarded away.

If knowledge is power, then don't keep it to yourself—give it away!

A couple of quick examples from my own life will illustrate the benefits and positive outcomes that result from becoming the unseen difference.

I once had a lovely lunch at The Baker Café in Encino, California. I loved talking with the restaurant's owner, who shared with me her experience leaving behind a corporate job to follow her dreams. After hearing her story, I encouraged her to continue pursuing those things most important to her. I also shared with her the dreams of one my daughters to someday open a Swiss-style bakery. A short time later, I sent her a copy of *The E-Myth Revisited*.[46] She soon sent me the following letter:

Dear Steve,

*What a surprise! Thank you so much for your kind gesture. I am thrilled to read **The E-Myth Revisited**. I enjoyed talking with you when you . . . had lunch here, and I very much appreciate the thoughtful gift.*

I hope your daughter pursues her dreams, and if I can help in any way, I'd be happy to hear from her.

Take care.
Best,

Sari
The Baker Café

By trying to become the unseen difference in Sari's life, I not only made her day a little brighter and hopefully shared some valuable information to help her in her own life pursuits, but I also found a potential mentor for my daughter.

We can all become the unseen difference by simply imparting and sharing, in a sincere manner, those things we feel will help others in what they're trying to accomplish. Sharing in this way, with no expectation of return, is ironic because often the greatest recipient of blessings is the one doing the sharing.

Another time, Ginger and I stayed at the Silver Fern, a motel in New Zealand. When it came time to check out, I began talking with the owners, Allan and Shirley. I soon learned that they had taken over the motel just a year or so earlier, and were now in the process of re-making the business. They were doing a great job.

Anytime I think about the hospitality industry, I am reminded of a book by Steven S. Little called *The Milkshake Moment*.[47] In this book, Little describes an experience he had while staying in a nice hotel. At the end of his day, he called room service and tried to order a milkshake. The person on the other end of the line very courteously informed Little that they could not provide him with a vanilla milkshake that evening. Little then asked if they had vanilla ice cream. Yes, they did. Did they have milk? Yes. Did they have a long spoon? Yes. The point of this anecdote is to emphasize the need to see beyond the accepted or the status quo, and to think creatively and logically in solving problems. I felt this book would be helpful to my friends, so I sent them a copy. Here is Allan's response:

Hi Steve,

What a fantastic surprise to arrive home after a few days' break and find the book waiting. I couldn't believe that you had remembered our chat after returning home, and had taken the time and made the effort to send me a copy. Thank you so much; it will take pride of place on my bookshelf (that is, as soon as I have reclaimed it from Shirley).

I only hope you make it back to New Zealand one day so we can continue our conversation and I can repay your generosity.

Trust all is well with life, both personal and business, and you enjoy your summer months.

Thank you once again. Kind regards,

Allan
Silver Fern, Rotorua

I originally received a copy of *The Milkshake Moment* from a friend acting as the unseen difference in my life. I read it and it enhanced my life, so when the opportunity arose, I became the unseen difference in the lives of Allan and Shirley, sharing that same book with them. I trust that someday Allan and Shirley will continue the cycle and pass it along to some other up and coming entrepreneur or young professional.

As we focus on being the unseen difference in the lives of others, a whole network of help and support is created. In this network, each individual learns and becomes better equipped to achieve their dreams and goals.

You lift me ⟶ and I'll lift thee ⟶ and we'll ascend together!

Now, remember the importance and the benefits of acting as the unseen difference, and "go and do thou likewise."[48]

Application and Relevance:

1. Understand that if your success doesn't help change the world for the better, it's value is greatly diminished.

2. Discover ways in which you can share the treasures you've learned in a humble and meaningful way.

3. Forget yourself and dedicate your success to benefitting others.

4. Become a person who makes an unseen difference and impacts the lives of many.

Chapter 10

Time To Sell

"A prudent question is one-half of wisdom."

- Francis Bacon

Chapter 10 image - *A welcome sight after a difficult trek, we arrive to rest, refocus, and think through our next steps.*

The Finish Line

At some point, any successful entrepreneur must consider his or her exit strategy. This represents the final step in entrepreneurial efforts—it is the finish line of all business ventures. An entrepreneur's ability to move away from his or her business and "retire" from the intimate involvement required throughout the business's formative years becomes the pinnacle of successful entrepreneurialism. Such a scenario indicates that the startup business has become strong and self-sustaining enough to survive its founder.

Of course, there can be many different types of finish lines, designed to fit the goals of each unique individual. For some, the quest may be to achieve a concrete and objective finish line such as selling the business. Others may be more interested in using one venture as a springboard to move into new ventures. For them, the concept of a finish line may be less clear-cut, as one finish line blends into the starting point of new ideas and activities.

Regardless of the exact shape your finish line takes, the concept is an important one to keep in mind. By giving yourself some sort of finish line, you help define the ultimate goal of your efforts. You set some standard toward which your business decisions and actions must work.

Defining your own personal finish line is largely a practice in self-examination; it's about asking yourself questions and answering them honestly. Ask yourself where you'd like to be in the next five years, the next ten years, and so on. Consider what type of future you most desire, and how you'd like your "retirement" to look. Do you want to step away entirely from the business world, move on to new projects, sell your business but stick around in another, perhaps less prominent position of guidance?

As you explore these types of questions, the answers you come up with will help shape exactly what your finish line will look like. Defining and then actually reaching a finish line requires long-term vision; it forces you to plan for the future and act effectively in the present.

Our Selling Experience: A Review Of Principles

I feel compelled to tell the story of my and Ginger's finish line in order to illustrate how the principles espoused throughout this book are real and relevant. From start to finish, the principles of spirituality, moral living, keeping covenants, following The Formula, and the many other ideas shared in this book have worked together as the compass for our business actions and decisions. We firmly believe it's because of these principles that our entrepreneurial endeavors have found success. These principles enabled us to cross our finish line.

As US–Reports continued to grow, Ginger and I eventually established the goal of selling the company to a trustworthy and honest buyer as our finish line. This goal required constant planning and hard work. It required us to look five years ahead and determine what the company should look like by then if it were to become attractive to a buyer. This vision then guided the way we set goals and made our plans.

In time, we began receiving phone calls and emails from various equity groups inquiring about our exit strategy. One day, we received a letter informing us of an upcoming seminar presented by a business brokerage firm. The seminar was intended to market the firm's services in helping business owners prepare to sell their companies. Ginger and I were immediately interested, so we prayed and asked whether or not we should attend. When the positive feelings of interest persisted, we decided to go.

After listening to the seminar, we hired the firm to prepare our company for a sale. In making our decision, we felt confident that we were acting in accordance with the spiritual promptings of our inner voices. We felt the timing was right for this sort of action, and we felt this was the right firm to help us in our efforts.

We quickly began learning the details of what it takes to sell a business. We learned the importance of having a strong "Platform," the comprehensive overview of the company including product descriptions, financial reports and analyses, and business plans along with accompanying financial forecasts for the next 2-3 years. We learned more about the metric, Earnings Before Income Tax and Depreciation (EBITDA), and how this statistic gives potential buyers the bottom line in terms of what they can expect to earn through purchasing a specific company. Through all of this, we discovered that US-Reports was not where it needed to be, and that it would take at least another two years of intense preparation in order to make it attractive to the right buyer.

The efforts of the next two years required us to make many wonderful changes. We experienced the power of change, the need for change, and the benefits of change in our lives. The preparation process required an even greater degree of discipline and long-term planning than ever before.

For example, when we were running the company without the anticipation of selling in the near future, as long as we were making a profit essential to sustain cash flow—usually more than 3% or 4%—we felt fine in distributing the amounts over this percentage to shareholders and associates. To maximize our selling price, however, we learned that the rule of thumb is to keep the company's EBITDA above 10%. Through learning this, we discovered that we should always be running the company according to this second guideline, as it keeps the business healthy and better prepared for a rainy day.

In the end, the process of preparing to sell was worthwhile, whether or not we ever actually sold, because of the lessons it taught our company and us.

Looking back on these years, I believe that our receiving the letter, attending the seminar, meeting and hiring the firm, and making the subsequent preparations suggested by this firm were not coincidences. These were all steps in the path laid for us by God. We see only a few steps ahead of us, but the God of Heaven sees the entire road. When we trust Him, and follow the divine inspiration of our spiritual promptings, we allow ourselves to walk the path He's provided. I've learned that His path leads us to knowledge, success, and happiness.

When our company was better prepared, the firm we had hired to sell our company lined up a host of interested visitors and potential buyers. Of all the folks we entertained, only one initially felt right. Both Ginger and I thought this company was exceptional, and we felt they met our criteria of trustworthiness and honesty. Their plan after purchasing the company was to replace me fairly quickly, but still allow me to stay involved as an "ambassador" for the company. The price we discussed was right, Ginger and I both felt strong personal and spiritual connections to the purchasing firm, and we were excited about the direction we were headed.

We worked with them in the due diligence process for a full year, and one week away from closing, while Ginger and I were eating lunch at our favorite hotdog joint, I received a call from the buyer. He told us that after talking one last time with all of the company's partners, there was a hesitant board member, and he would have to back out of the deal.

We were shocked and dismayed. Remember how I felt midway through the lawsuit we faced when first starting our company?

I felt just as exhausted after realizing the yearlong process of due diligence now amounted to nothing. We were disappointed. We didn't understand why this sale hadn't gone through, but again, all we could do was trust the Lord and do our best to live according to the covenants we had made with Him.

After this experience, we decided to simply continue running US–Reports ourselves and stop entertaining sales proposals. It was during the years immediately following this failed sales attempt that we began the company-wide charity donations program described earlier. This became a crucial component of the culture at US–Reports, and really helped provide the fine-tuned details regarding its corporate identity. Suddenly, Ginger and I were thankful that this first sale hadn't gone through—if it had, we would never have been able to establish the principle of giving back as a defining attribute of our company.

Three years after the first sales attempt, and shortly after US–Reports' donations program was firmly in place, we received an unexpected call from a potential client who wanted to discuss a national contract with our company. As we continued talking, their interest in US–Reports increased until the initial idea of a national contract grew into an interest in purchasing US–Reports altogether.

Eventually the time came to give a formal sales presentation to this firm. As I prepared for this important event, I read Guy Kawasaki's *The Art of the Start*.[49] I followed every step outlined in his chapter, "The Art of Pitching." Ginger and I felt the pitch was perfectly constructed, and well delivered, and within two weeks they made an offer to buy US–Reports.

Those who have been down this road will understand the mix of emotions that come with letting go of something you've built and cared about for over 20 years. Even though we still believed the timing was right to sell our company, we also felt some reservations as we looked over the proposed offer. Although we didn't know exactly what caused these uneasy feelings, we didn't want to ignore whatever our inner voices were trying to tell us, so we acted on faith and declined the offer.

A short three months later, while participating in a conference at BYU-Hawaii, Ginger and I were introduced to Bill Child, whose entrepreneurial successes had recently been documented in the book, *How to Build a Business Warren Buffett Would Buy*, by Jeff Benedict.[50] On the way home from the conference, I read the book and immediately realized that Bill's business philosophies and selling criteria mirrored my own.

In particular, I was inspired by Bill's focus on finding a buyer who would maintain and protect the fundamental business principles most important to him. As a result, Ginger and I adopted three of Bill's requirements for selling, and added them to our own criteria:

1. A buyer must protect our family and associates. Many times, an equity group will buy a company, gut it, and push for hard market increases so they can turn around and re-sell it within 5 years. In these situations, they really don't care about the people and the employees involved. Bill sold to Warren Buffett because of his reputation for keeping the purchased business and its personnel intact. We also felt this to be a deeply important requirement for selling our business—the group of associates and employees we had built up over the years was certainly important enough for us to protect.

2. Honoring the Sabbath Day was important to Bill, and he made this a requirement for any potential buyer. We shared this same commitment.

3. When Bill sold R.C. Willey Home Furnishings, he was allowed to stay on and participate in the day-to-day activities and guidance of the business after the sale. He was more than an "ambassador" for his former company, and Buffett counted on him to continue leading the business to success. This was the type of role Ginger and I decided we wanted to maintain with our company as well.

While these specific stipulations may or may not make your list of selling requirements, the lesson here is to ponder what fundamental principles are most important to you and your business. Don't be afraid to require that any potential buyer contractually promise to maintain and protect these important principles. The greatest business success results from moral, service-oriented living, so don't let all your hard work go by the wayside in the final moment. Stand up for the principles important to you and make their maintenance actual requirements for anybody interested in buying your company.

Some questions to ask yourself when trying to establish your requirements for selling are:

- What involvement do you desire after the sale, and how will you ensure that it happens? As a note, if you desire to continue involvement with the company, be prepared for a shift in dynamics. Things will change and decisions will be made that you're no longer in charge of. Relationships with employees and associates may change. There can be some real challenges when you remain involved with your company after selling it, but there can also be some deeply rewarding experiences as you witness your company continue to grow and progress in brand new ways.

- How will you protect your associates, the team that "got you there" in the first place?

- How will your company's culture be protected, and how will you keep the company from morphing into another empire with an entirely different identity?

- Does the sales contract reflect the exit strategy that's best for you, your family, and your future?

- What selling price is right? How much is "enough?" Will the sale set you up with income sufficient for retirement? Will it allow you to fund your philanthropy work and create the future lifestyle of service you desire? Striking the right balance between having enough to provide for your needs plus a little extra, the greatest amount you think your business is worth, and the greatest amount the buyer's willing to pay can be tricky. My advice is to not be greedy.

After this important moment of learning and inspiration, I immediately sent Benedict's book to the buyer we had recently turned down. I asked them to read it and told them, "If you're still interested, this is exactly how I would want to proceed."

They read the book, and within two months the deal was finalized. We sold our company to the world's largest independent insurance broker, and by requiring that our most important business principles remained intact, were able to ensure that US–Reports—the company that meant so much to us—would continue on in the direction we'd always intended it to, safe in the hands of trustworthy owners.

Consider all the seeming coincidences that led to the selling of our company:

1. The invitation to attend a meeting hosted by a business brokerage firm.

2. Two years of preparation that enhanced our company, increased our efficiency and discipline, and taught us the nuances of the selling process.

3. A failed sales attempt—initially a discouragement—actually gave us the time to implement a policy of giving back, which became the capstone to our company's identity.

4. After reading Guy Kawasaki's book and meeting Bill Child, Ginger and I discovered the missing pieces required to make the sale of our company fully fit our desires. We learned the importance of requiring any potential buyer to maintain our company's fundamental philosophies even after the sale is complete.

5. Once our company's identity had been solidified and completed, and we had thoroughly strategized how we wanted the selling of our company to occur, the right buyer contacted us, and the deal was completed. Through all of this, we again learned the importance of letting God guide our lives according to His will and His timetable. He always prepares the path, and we must be ready to follow His will even if we don't fully understand it.

Obviously there are no coincidences. A person of faith cannot fail to see the hand of God in a series of events such as this. There are many lessons to be learned in the process of a business exit strategy. For those desiring to embark on the process of selling your business, I would encourage you to consider the following:

Critical Points Before Selling

Know the reasons why you desire to sell—do they fit The Formula?

Don't put your own timetable on the process; allow your inner voice of inspiration to be heard over your personal desires.

Once your desires are aligned with Deity and you're willing to accept God's timing, the doors of opportunity will be opened.

For Ginger and I, there were several reasons we desired to sell our business. The personal objectives we hoped to achieve through selling fit into The Formula, as the sale provided greater opportunities for us to serve and give back to the good causes with which we were engaged. Selling our company also provided additional strength and benefit for US–Reports, allowing it to be backed by over a billion dollars in times of economic uncertainty. In turn, this greater financial security allowed our close business associates and employees to continue progressing and growing in their own efforts.

Although the process of preparing to sell, meeting with potential buyers, figuring out exactly what we wanted from a sale, and finally landing a deal was a long and grueling one, the lessons of patience, trust, and faith these experiences taught us couldn't have been learned any other way. Once again, we learned to set aside our own timetables, and to trust God's guidance. The miracles we experienced as we allowed things to develop according to His timing increased our faith in Him.

After all the components of the sale finally came together, we were blessed to sell our beloved company to a man who shares our desire to live according to the commandments of God. Although we don't share the exact same religion, we feel a special connection as individuals of faith who are working hard to live according to the moral codes we've been taught. I am grateful for the central role played by the hand of God in connecting our paths.

Application and Relevance:

1. It's important to establish your finish line. This lends continued direction and motivation to all your efforts.

2. Selling a business requires long term preparation—there are no short cuts.

3. Implement a giving back program long before attempting to sell your company. When your heart is right, God's timing will be revealed.

4. Hire an outside firm to sell your company. Whether or not you actually sell, this process will make your company better.

5. Selling a business should be a practice in self-examination. Before selling, you must decide what your desired outcomes are for your family, work associates, and yourself. In particular, ask yourself:

    a. Why am I selling?
    b. Why do I feel that now is the right time?
    c. Do I want to "retire?"
    d. Will I continue on with the company or leave the day it sells?

e. How will a sale affect my family and associates?

f. Where do I see myself five years after selling?

g. Where does God see me at this same time?

Chapter 11

The New Zealand Experience

"Before Launching Leaders, I did not believe my dreams were possible."

- Yi-Han Wu,

2011 Launching Leaders participant and winner of Entrepreneurial Plan Competition

Chapter 11 image - A Maori carved face tells intricate stories of family, culture, tradition, and future potential.

Launching Leaders

As described in previous chapters, Ginger and I adopted James Ritchie as our mentor 30 years ago. Since then, his advice and guidance has inculcated in our minds the importance of such concepts as The Formula, adopting effective mentors, Financial Fitness, and developing a Personal Constitution.

After applying these concepts to our lives and experiencing the powerful impacts they've made, it was decided in April 2010 that these principles of success should be organized into a curriculum and taught to the world. Under the direction and vision of James Ritchie, Ginger and I participated in a small roundtable comprised of several other successful entrepreneurs, and together, we created Launching Leaders.

Launching Leaders is a 12-week intensive career-training and personal development program aimed at providing the skills, knowledge, and support needed by young people to put into action their business, professional, or entrepreneurial ideas. The principles and ideas discussed in this book are the same ones taught in Launching Leaders.

At the start of the program, participants are paired with a carefully and specifically chosen mentor. This mentor then serves as the student's support throughout the program, and continues to provide help, feedback, advice, and teaching long after the program ends— within the model of Launching Leaders, mentoring is a lifelong relationship. Once each student is paired with the appropriate mentor, they then select a course of study: Career Development, Life Plans, or Entrepreneurial Endeavors.

Regardless of the field of study chosen, the centerpiece of Launching Leaders is its unique curriculum. In designing it, our goal was to combine spiritual teachings with concrete business principles in order to deliver an education aimed at helping students achieve overall life success, instead of only financial success. In everything Launching Leaders teaches, we recognize the bigger picture of personal and spiritual growth. We all believe that business achievement is only one piece in the making of a truly happy, truly content, and truly successful individual.

In putting together the curriculum of Launching Leaders, we received gracious permission from Guy Kawasaki to teach the principles of his book, *The Art of The Start,* to which we added a new spiritual component.[51] Stephen R. Covey also gave us permission to use concepts found in *Great Work, Great Career,* and we used material from Jim Collins' book, *Good to Great.*[52] James Ritchie's lecture series, focusing on The Formula, the importance of mentors, Financial Fitness, and the Personal Constitution, tie all these ideas and information together into a single powerful seminar on life success.

After our group built the program's curriculum, James Ritchie felt that Launching Leaders should begin its operation working with young adults in New Zealand. He and his wife had previously taught Institute of Religion classes in this area, and felt strongly that this country would provide the best testing ground for the new program. After the idea had been suggested to the rest of the organizers, we all agreed that it felt right, and so, beginning in 2011, Launching Leaders taught its first groups of students.

The introduction of these first Launching Leaders sessions was facilitated in large part by Terry and Mary Pitts, who lived in New Zealand for six months to oversee final preparations and ensure that the program got off to a strong start. Looking back, it's clear that Terry and Mary were just the right people to fill this crucial role. Once again, there are no coincidences—Terry and Mary are so selfless, so gifted, and so perfect for the work needed to launch this program.

Along with them, local mentors and leaders Jay Seymour, Moses Armstrong, and Richard Ball also put in countless hours of volunteer effort to ensure a successful start for Launching Leaders.

Since its first sessions in New Zealand, Launching Leaders has begun teaching in other parts of the world, including the United States. As the program continues to teach its powerful perspectives on what constitutes success and how one may attain this success, we've seen the program's lessons make significant changes in the lives of its participants.

One of the most consistently meaningful ideas conveyed to students is the concept that not only is it possible to become successful financially while still remaining a spiritually-grounded and loving individual, but that these two goals actually work together in complete symbiosis. In fact, one of the primary underlying beliefs of Launching Leaders is that success is defined as a congruency between spiritual and business activity, and that when such congruency is achieved, people will discover the greatest degree of prosperity, success, and happiness.

Although no metrics tracking the real-world successes of Launching Leaders graduates are included here, suffice it to say that a number of profitable businesses have been created, numerous careers have been enhanced, and many wandering young adults have found anchors for their lives thanks to the teachings of Launching Leaders.

As an example, when Neum Muliaumasealii began learning how to establish a life plan for himself, he left his past life of crime, voluntarily confessed to local authorities, and stood tall as he accepted the consequences of his misdeeds in the courtroom. Since then, Neum has devoted his whole heart toward utilizing the principles he learned in Launching Leaders and is working tirelessly to build a meaningful career that will enable him to give back and serve others. So it is that

Launching Leaders encourages individuals to bury the duplicitous life and begin a new path of success and purpose.

There are many more stories and experiences just as dramatic and heart-warming as Neum's. Each one stands as a living testimony to the efficacy and power of the ideas taught both in this book and in Launching Leaders. The following section includes a series of these stories, told by the Launching Leaders organizers, teachers, mentors, and graduates who lived them. In addition, we have also interviewed more than 25 alumni, mentors, and leaders of the program, and their experiences are documented in a supplemental DVD, available at theministryofbusiness.com. Together, these stories provide compelling evidence that the principles taught in both Launching Leaders and *The Ministry of Business* have the ability to significantly and positively change the lives of anybody willing to implement them into their everyday lives.

Proof Of Concept: Words From Launching Leaders Participants

Terry and Mary Pitts
Launching Leaders Founding Members

My wife, Mary, and I were asked to volunteer for six months to oversee the New Zealand launch of Launching Leaders. Throughout 2011, the program taught three intakes (registrations of up to 60 young adults) of students in both the Auckland and Hamilton areas.

One of the truly incredible things our students gained from learning the principles of Launching Leaders was a new and definite purpose and direction for their lives. As young adults, many of our students were simultaneously enrolled in university. They had to work especially hard to keep up with the demands of both curriculums, but by putting forth the effort to complete the Launching Leaders program, they learned spiritual and personal lessons they could not have gained anywhere else.

The majority of our students were at one of those junctures when numerous life paths converge and possibilities seem limitless. They were at that point when they were trying to figure out who they are, what they want to become, and what sorts of careers and professional paths they want to pursue. We've all been at these types of crossroads, and we all understand the mixture of excitement and worry these times bring about. We feel excited by the feeling that there are so many possible directions for life, but worried and confused over actually deciding which direction is right for us.

Struggling with these life decisions, our students benefited greatly from the concept of the Personal Constitution. Learning to be introspective, and to really check in with themselves in terms of what they wanted to become and how well they were progressing toward their goals really became a powerful life tool. I watched as many of these young adults learned to face their worries with optimism and confidence, sure that their Personal Constitutions would serve as trustworthy life compasses.

In particular, I remember one student who was excited about being enrolled in the program, but didn't know which course of study to focus on. After hearing a mentor give a "Life Plan" presentation—in which the mentor talked about his experiences formulating a 25-year plan for himself and then making this plan attainable through regularly setting smaller, incremental goals—this student knew that lesson was exactly what she needed at that point in her life. She ended up focusing on the Life Plan course of study, and at graduation, her new air of calm and composed confidence amazed me. Although she still didn't know exactly what she wanted to do as a career, she talked about now having the tools needed to accelerate her life forward.

One of the things I've been repeatedly moved by is the way the mentors are themselves affected by interacting with students. As Mary and I worked to organize the very first session of Launching Leaders, we had a mentor who nearly backed out. He was too busy at the moment with his own professional life, he told us. After some discussion, he finally agreed to stay on with the program, but was still unsure of how committed he would be once the program finally began.

Well, within the first couple weeks of working with his assigned students, this mentor fell completely in love with being a mentor. He had never before experienced providing this type of service and help. Mentoring was a truly unique experience for him. It allowed him to give back to others in a very meaningful way while simultaneously using the professional and entrepreneurial know-how he'd worked so hard to acquire and which had helped him gain success in the business world. This mentor became so deeply committed to his students that he still maintains regular contact with them, continuing to provide valuable help and advice.

Focusing on this type of well-rounded approach to business—taking into consideration solid financial and business practices as well as spiritual and moral principles—has shown me just how great the potential of every single individual really is. When we work together to foster feelings of service-oriented cooperation, great things can happen. They have already happened through Launching Leaders, and they will continue to happen as people around the world espouse the principles of Launching Leaders and *The Ministry of Business*.

Josh Roa
Launching Leaders Alumni; Auckland, New Zealand

My father, who had served as a mentor for the program, introduced me to Launching Leaders at a really difficult time in my life. I had some good ideas for businesses that I wanted to start, but I just couldn't seem to get any of them to really move forward. This was frustrating, but even worse was the fact that my marriage wasn't going well. We were unhappy at home, and it felt like my wife and I had somehow stopped communicating. When my dad suggested I enroll in Launching Leaders, I figured it couldn't hurt anything, so I signed up and started working with a mentor. Soon, things started falling into place and my life looked like it was beginning to move in a positive direction.

One of the biggest things Launching Leaders stressed was the importance of joining together religious standards and business principles in order to be the same person no matter where we may be or with whom we may be working. The teachers and mentors taught me how to bridge the gap between the spiritual values I had kind of given up on and the effective business principles I was beginning to learn. I started to understand that by marrying the spiritual and the business, I would have a stronger base for all aspects of my life.

Early on in the program, I made a personal commitment to re-dedicate myself to the spiritual and religious teachings I had learned growing up, but which I had kind of abandoned. Just as I began focusing more on this side of my life, great things started happening in the business side of my life. I had been working on an idea to somehow streamline the used car buying process by providing cheaper, more accessible mechanic reports to potential buyers. I felt good about the idea, but had run into a wall when I couldn't obtain some critical pieces of data that I needed to really put my idea into action. I'd been stuck, sitting on my idea for nine to twelve months. Shortly after I began focusing more on my spiritual life, I suddenly received a phone call from a contact that was able to arrange an interview with the people who ultimately gave me all the information I needed to move my idea forward. I fully view this breakthrough as a blessing for following and living my newly revived covenants with God—nothing's coincidental.

While all this was certainly exciting, the changes taking place within my family were even more meaningful to me. I understand now that one of the biggest things weakening my marriage was my inability to communicate effectively with my wife. There were many times that I didn't talk to her about our financial situation. I felt like anything dealing with money was my job to handle as the husband, and when things weren't going well, I was reluctant to tell her anything. This lack of communication began eating away at our entire relationship.

After learning the importance of being transparent with our spouses, I finally started talking candidly and honestly with my wife. It was difficult at first, but we were able to talk about our weaknesses as a family, and we started coming up with plans for fixing these weaknesses. Now that I've tried to focus on communicating and being transparent in all that I do, I've got a much stronger relationship with my wife. She's noticed that my communication skills have dramatically improved, and this is helping our family grow stronger.

As a result of bridging the chasm between my spiritual life and my business life, I've experienced great blessings professionally, personally, and especially with my family. Where I used to feel a bleak sense of pessimism and frustration, I now feel hope and positivity. When I meet people, I'm more confident because I now know there's something greater behind what I'm doing with my life. I feel much more empowered because I understand what it takes to be a successful person—not just a successful entrepreneur or businessman—but a successful all-around individual. In a very real way, the things I learned from Launching Leaders saved my life and the life of my family.

Johnson McKay
Original Mentor for Launching Leaders in New Zealand

The principles taught by Launching Leaders have had a profound impact on my life, both personally and as a mentor.

I grew up in a very poor family—you probably couldn't be poorer in New Zealand than my family was. Growing up this way, I'd never considered going to university; my first management position was mind blowing to my family and me.

Generally, this is also true of anybody living in a lower income society. In the minds of people in these circumstances, university isn't an option—they're not even thinking about it—and the prospect of becoming a manager isn't considered. So it's a massive cultural shift for anyone from a low income society to conclude for themselves that they can get a job, they can go to university, they can get married, and they can be successful and happy. Yet these are the very things taught by Launching Leaders.

By the time I became engaged with Launching Leaders as a teacher and a mentor, I had built a successful business, but I still wasn't sure if it was truly my life's work. I didn't want to put 60 years into this business only to realize that it wasn't really what I was intended to do with my life. The opportunity to serve as a mentor in the Launching Leaders program provided a concrete and tangible way for me to use business success as a means of serving others, and as such, helped address some of my concerns that I may not be pursuing my true life's work.

As a mentor, I try to teach young people the same lessons I've learned. I encourage them to broaden their horizons of who they are and what their potential is, while at the same time trying to become very focused on what God has blessed them with that will unlock this potential. I try to help the young people I work with understand the fundamental message of Launching Leaders: set big goals, plan what's necessary for their accomplishment, and work with God to achieve them.

Serving as a mentor has also changed my perspective on what it means to serve God. It means providing practical, tangible help to people who need it now. It's not just about teaching doctrine and attending church; it's about practical, real help. I'd never considered that God might have a use for my talents in these kinds of ways.

Ultimately, serving as a mentor has reinforced the importance of following The Formula. My favorite part of The Formula is its focus on preparing to serve. The idea that the focal point of your entire life's work is to achieve a state where there are no obstacles to completely devoting yourself to serving others was a standard I hadn't ever considered attainable by people like myself. This final step provides the ultimate end to all our actions and goals, and it's the real power behind The Formula.

Through living and teaching these concepts, I've learned that as we make service the guiding principle of our goals, actions, and decisions, we can become instruments in God's hands. It's amazing just how much God can do with our simple talents.

Chelsea Turner
Launching Leaders Alumni; Auckland, New Zealand

When I attended Launching Leaders, I signed up for the Career Development course of study. In my classes, I learned to be bold in my quest to make a positive impact in my job, my family, and my community.

The capstone to this program was developing a "Contribution Statement" that would outline specific ideas and actions I would pursue in my career that would allow me to meet my personal goals.[53] My Contribution Statement was a plan describing exactly what I would do to make a meaningful impact in my profession.

The Contribution Statement I put together was well received by my Launching Leaders teachers and mentor. After graduating from the program, I ended up using this statement to create a formal presentation, which I then gave to the CEO of the communications company I work for. He really liked my ideas, and a few months after the presentation, the entire company underwent a significant re-structuring that was directly influenced by my presentation.

Since these changes, the company's operations are more closely aligned with the model I proposed, and it's now much more focused on customer service and satisfaction. The company isn't functioning exactly according to my suggestions, but I'm happy to say that the changes it has made have all been a result of my meeting with the CEO.

The lessons I learned in Launching Leaders, and the support I've received from teachers and mentors have made a life-changing impact on me. Learning how to set goals, make plans, and put into practice powerful business ideas has been an awesome ride and an incredible experience.

Now that I have a more solid vision of the types of positive changes and impacts I can make on the world around me, I have greater motivation to work hard and be proactive in all facets of life.

___

Tu'u Singsam
Launching Leaders Alumni; Auckland, New Zealand

The Launching Leaders principles affirmed that God has given me special and unique talents and abilities. I learned that because of this, I have great potential to succeed not only in my professional life, but also as an individual working to make a positive impact on the world around me.

These concepts became especially clear when I wrote my Personal Constitution and began applying it to my career. With this guidance, I was able to align spiritual and ethical principles with principles for effectiveness in my employment. These became deeply connected in my everyday life.

A short time after graduating from Launching Leaders, I had feelings of great peace as I was interviewed for a promotion. Instead of feeling all the tension, worry, and pressure that often goes along with these types of interviews, I felt calm, content, and confident because I actually didn't mind whether or not I got the promotion. What was more important to me was the fact that I was beginning to understand God's will for my life, and I felt that I was beginning to live my life in accordance with this will. As long as my life was in line with God, I had faith that whatever happened would somehow work out in the end.

As a result of my calm confidence and my new perspective on life and work, the interview went extremely well. I was soon offered a promotion, and I happily accepted.

In my opinion, although Launching Leaders certainly provides the tools to become a highly successful professional, it's really not about getting the promotion or making a lot of money. It's about discovering your divine purpose and then doing all you can to further that purpose, to make a difference in the lives of others, and to serve God wherever, however, and whenever He directs you to serve.

The Abundant Life

Teaching in New Zealand, and working with many of the country's native Maori culture, has highlighted some especially powerful aspects of what *The Ministry of Business* is really trying to teach. Among the Maori, community is deeply important. There are also some particularly strong cultural attitudes toward money in which financial success is often interpreted as inherently and fundamentally opposed to the ideal of a humble, community-oriented, and serving lifestyle.

As we began teaching through Launching Leaders, we sensed some conflicting feelings among our students regarding money, professional achievement, and maintaining a culturally appropriate personal lifestyle. As we taught that it is indeed possible to maintain an honest, upright, and service-oriented lifestyle while also following the dreams of entrepreneurial and financial success, we saw many of our students' mindsets drastically transform. By focusing on the way a positive and spiritual life improves one's business efforts, and highlighting the fact that greater financial success then makes it even easier to give back to the community in meaningful ways, a new sense of hope was born.

As I've thought about this experience, the need for a new term to encompass both financial success and honorable living has become clear. I have since adopted the phrase, "the abundant life," to describe this state of all-around successful living.

Throughout my life experiences of learning, working, starting businesses, and teaching the things most important to me, I've discovered that the objective of being self-reliant and working hard is not enjoying the comforts of life as much as it is building up a life of abundance through the living of correct principles.

Thomas S. Monson, president of the LDS church, has said:

"The abundant life does not consist of a glut of luxury. It does not make itself content with commercially produced pleasure, the nightclub idea of what is a good time, mistaking it for joy and happiness. On the contrary, obedience to law, respect for others, mastery of self, joy in service—these constitute the abundant life."[54]

As President Monson has stated, the abundant life has much more to do with the principles we let govern our life than it does the material objects we amass. William James put this idea another way when he wrote: "The greatest revolution of our generation is the discovery that human beings, by changing the inner attitudes of their minds, can change the outer aspects of their lives."[55] This is an especially productive way of thinking, as it places all the emphasis on our own behavior, beliefs, and attitudes—those things we have complete control over.

Following are three guidelines to help us focus on those things in life we can control. By choosing to take charge of these parts of our lives, we are able to more effectively pursue the abundant life:

Time

Focus a good deal of time each day on improving the life of someone else; measure your success by this accomplishment.

Graciousness

Strive to cloak your actions with graciousness—gratitude is a great soil in which to plant the seeds of abundance.

Attitude

So much of the outcome of our lives is the result of our positive approach; strive to live in an attitude that creates altitude and helps you rise above the negative influences of the world.

The principles comprising *The Ministry of Business* and the abundant life are intrinsically intertwined. This is the basic message of this book, and this is exactly what we saw so clearly in the success of Launching Leaders in New Zealand.

Application and Relevance:

1. The ideas expounded in this book really work; the success of Launching Leaders in New Zealand was proof of this beyond our own lives.

2. Any limiting circumstances can be overcome through the implementation of correct principles.

3. It's a lie that one cannot live a morally upstanding life while at the same time achieving financial wealth. In fact, true joy is found when these two are congruent.

4. The quest of both Launching Leaders and *The Ministry of Business* is to help you enjoy the abundant life: not just the money and wealth of success, but the appropriate use of your time, talents, and gifts to bless the lives of others.

Chapter 12

Final Thoughts

"The wilderness can be a lonely place. Many of us try to escape the wilderness and God's plan of testing for our lives. We try to minister only in our natural strength as Moses once did (Exodus 2:11-15). Such ministry is useless. I think I would rather spend forty years in the wilderness and minister only one day in the Lord's strength, than to spend one day in the wilderness and minister forty years in my own strength."

- Jim Gerrish

Chapter 12 image - While attaining the goal should remain your primary focus, remember that travelling the pathway to this goal is what creates greatness.

When Ginger and I interviewed and filmed the mentors, students, and leaders of Launching Leaders in New Zealand, my final question to each individual was: "Any final thoughts?" In this moment of reflection, gratitude filled their hearts, and in nearly every instance, they expressed, with great emotion, appreciation for the impact the principles of Launching Leaders has had in their lives.[56]

Ginger and I feel the exact same way. Although we didn't necessarily learn these principles in an organized classroom, they have been taught to us in one way or another and we have lived them. We have lived everything taught by Launching Leaders; we have lived *The Ministry of Business*.

I hope you've felt a connection to the journey of hope and enlightenment documented in this book. Thirty years ago, Ginger and I would never have imagined that becoming students to a mentor would change the entire course of our lives, that we could also become mentors, that we could make a difference and give back to others. I would never have imagined that the principles comprising *The Ministry of Business* would be able to positively affect hundreds of folks—from New Zealand to Virginia, from Canada to Chile, and across the entire globe—just as they have affected us.

There is nary a day that goes by that we don't hear from someone we mentored in Launching Leaders, or someone we connected with while on the journey of organizing and implementing the program. We receive questions, comments, notes of thanks, and personal letters that have become sacred to us. We've talked with literally hundreds of people involved in this work that have had the same delightful experiences we've had. This has made clear to Ginger and I that our experiences are not unique; they are the experiences available to anybody willing to live according to the principles of *The Ministry of Business*.

We have not kept metrics regarding the number of businesses started, the opportunities made possible, or the lives changed as a result of organized efforts to teach these concepts. We do know, however, that many are now living The Formula and are working hard to make their marks in the world. They are giving back. Like a little snowball rolling down the mountainside, the overall impact of these principles grows bigger every day. There is a gathering of faithful souls who have discovered, and who are continuing to discover, the power of living according to what they know to be true.

I hope this book serves as a witness to the fact that all who live can make a difference for good. You don't have to be an acclaimed superstar to stand as an ensign. You don't have to "make it big" before you can make your own positive mark on this world. Recognizing the divinity within you and realizing your divine potential are fundamental pieces of your identity as a human being. A strong understanding of these truths will be attained by living what you know, listening to and acting upon the promptings of your inner voice, trusting God's timing in your life, and experiencing the peace that comes from this process.

One of the issues facing our day is the increasingly hedonistic attitude of many young adults. Living lives devoted to the pursuit of pleasure and self-gratification, these individuals focus on whatever whims bring instant satisfaction. Their sole concern is themselves and their own private happiness. Sadly, this focus can often lead to addictions and personal practices that destroy lives.

The solution to this hedonism is building a life focused on making and living according to covenants with God, since such covenants are largely aimed at living morally upright lives, providing service, and giving back to others. I hope the teachings of this book will contribute to breaking the yoke of selfishness by providing life-long answers and practices that will uplift, inspire, and empower.

Let me conclude with one final thought. The photo above is many years old. It's a picture of my Dad teaching one of my sons to fish. Their eyes are focused on the fly in the stream. Fly-fishing is a game of patience, and anticipation is great while watching a trout approach the fly. There is an element of the unknown in this sport, and yet, the experience of trying to catch a fish brings smiles to both their faces. There is joy in striving to accomplish their goal.

My Dad is teaching my son that there are rules of successful fishing, and when we abide by these rules, we will catch the fish. The whole process of learning the rules, working hard to follow them, and eventually experiencing success is truly meaningful and empowering.

I've had a strong desire to somehow weave my Dad into this book, and this is the perfect way to do so. He has since passed on, and now fishes in heavenly lakes. But the legacy he left on Earth continues. He never knew The Formula, yet he lived it. He never had a Personal

Constitution, but he still lived as if he had written one. He was never taught the principle of giving back, but he was always a generous man.

How is it that he could achieve all of this? He, too, had mentors. The laws taught in this book are grounded so fundamentally in what is right and true, that they create a natural path to success for anybody willing to listen, regardless of how, when, or where a person learns them.

Whether resulting from this book or as a natural consequence of doing the right thing at the right time, may hope abound in your life and may your journey take you to the Promised Land.

Application and Relevance:

1. The experiences and success stories shared in this book are not unique. They are available to anybody willing to learn and live according to the principles of *The Ministry of Business*.

2. Like fly-fishing, success is attained by learning the rules required to achieve a goal and then working hard to abide by these rules.

3. *The Ministry of Business* outlines a ministry of success and hope. As you experience the success these concepts bring into your life, share what you've learned with others. This is the ultimate cycle of success.

Afterword

"You can't connect the dots looking forward, you can only connect them looking backwards."

- Steve Jobs[57]

When I look back over our life together, I can truly see God's hand in directing and supporting Steve and me. I have often pondered whether or not our life story is all that different or unique from the stories of others, and if so, what makes it unique. I've reached the conclusion that, in many ways, our story is one experienced by many other couples. It's a story in which hopes and dreams are shared. A story in which both partners do whatever it takes to make those dreams a reality.

As I've continued reflecting on our life story, I truly believe that what made the difference for us was learning all the principles that have been discussed in this book. Steve and I were fortunate to meet and be mentored by James Ritchie early on in our marriage. We were smart enough to recognize a great thing when it came along, and then work hard to implement into our lives what he taught us. From there, we continued searching out and learning other truths, adding them to those we had already grown to love.

Through learning these lessons and living these experiences, I have come to know that the pieces of my life can be arranged in many different ways. If I am left to myself, I can arrange these pieces to form a decent picture. However, if I work with God, allowing Him to be the ultimate artist, the picture can become magnificent—something I would never even have considered possible.

As Steve and I have tried to let God become the artist of our life story, we've experienced wonderful things. We certainly haven't been perfect, and there are still times when we try to operate according to our wills, ideas, and schedules instead of God's, but I believe our efforts have been blessed.

Throughout our marriage, we both have had total and equal buy-in regarding what we wanted our future life to look like. We knew from day one that we wanted to raise our family and then serve together to make a difference in the lives of others. Discovering how we were to get there, and what that road would look like has been the fun part.

Early on, we both were working in our own unique roles. Steve was working as manager of an office and I was taking care of things at home. After the fateful trip to Kansas City, we felt strongly about starting our own company, and it became fun to consider these new possibilities together. It was a melding of our unique personal strengths. We were able to create a brand new business. We brainstormed, rolled up our sleeves, and got to work, doing anything and everything we could to make things happen.

In life and in business, a great partnership is one that evolves and adapts as life changes. When we first started our business, we had an eight-year-old, a six-year-old, and a pair of 18-month-old twins. Our lives were busy, and just as we were establishing our first office and settling into a new rhythm, Steve was served with the lawsuit. Dealing with this required him to live away from home for most of each month.

I felt very conflicted. Steve staying and working in southern California wasn't an option. This required me to oversee things at the office, yet we had four young children at home. I needed to be two places at one time—there simply wasn't enough of me to go around.

I knew that God had directed us to "jump off the cliff" and start this business. I also knew that He never sets His children up to fail, and that if we will follow Him, trusting in the spiritual promptings we receive, somehow a way will open up, even if we can't see it at the time. I humbly approached God in prayer and told Him of my dilemma. I explained my need to care for our children and our business at the same time. I explained my need to somehow multiply myself, and asked Him for help in figuring out a way to do all that was required of me.

A few days later I was talking to my sister on the phone. She told me she had recently hired a young woman to help her around the house, and that she might also be able to help me find a nanny if I was interested. This was such a foreign concept to me that at first I balked at the idea. Having a nanny help take care of my kids was something I had never even considered. In some ways, I felt having a nanny was actually contrary to my natural instincts as a mother. Yet I also knew I had asked God to help me, and there was such a sweet feeling that accompanied this idea that—despite my personal misgivings—I explored this possibility.

It only took two phone calls to get in touch with Judith Mueller. It was truly amazing how quickly we bonded and how well everything fell into place for her to come to the U.S. from her native Switzerland to live with us. Judy immediately became my extra hands, arms, and heart. My family and I love Judy, and to this day, she holds a special place in our lives. Her coming to live with us allowed me to get back to work at the office and help grow the business during this critical time, while feeling confident that all was well at home. Steve and I were so fortunate and blessed to find someone like Judy willing to help us.

As our children grew up, US–Reports was always a family business. We ate, drank, and slept it. We talked around the dinner table about our successes, our concerns, and our future plans. It seemed like every vacation we took was centered on inspections and audits. Often times, when Steve had a job to complete somewhere, we'd turn his trip into a family activity. While he performed his inspections, the children and I would play at a park until he finished and we could go do something fun together.

Having our family around was a constant part of how we ran our business, and we loved it! I remember holding board meetings with a crib in the corner for our youngest to nap in while we talked. We had such grand adventures during the early days of US–Reports, and these adventures eventually led us to Fort Collins, Colorado, where we continued raising our little family and our business.

Once we had several offices set up and the company's staffing needs were fully met, it was a natural transition for me to ease out of the business to focus on the increasing needs of our growing children. The new demands of our ever-changing family required the attention of a full-time mom, so that's where I devoted myself.

I have been blessed to be able to be at home with our children and still be involved on an intimate level with the workings of our company. I have had the flexibility to shift back and forth as needed, and to adjust my level of involvement in these important life endeavors. Looking back, I fully realize this was only possible because of God's love and involvement in our lives. He took my family's life story in unforeseen directions and created beautiful pictures we never anticipated. Of course, success is never easy, and attempting to juggle family life and business life is always a non-stop struggle. But with God's help all things become possible.

I realize what a unique experience partnering with my husband has been. I know that my role was vital in stabilizing our family and assisting my husband in our business. We have come to rely on and trust each other completely. Because we've always shared everything, when our children grew up and left home, it felt completely natural for us to continue growing together to fill new roles in life. Now, I love being able to devote as much time as I want toward working with Steve in our new pursuits. Together, we lecture, mentor, and teach others in an effort to give back and serve.

When I look back and connect the dots of our life, I recognize that applying the principles of *The Ministry of Business* has made all the difference. These principles are true and correct, and they will benefit anyone who wants to succeed in life and be truly happy. In the end, while the story of my and Steve's life is certainly our own, I've reached the conclusion that it's not entirely unique or exclusively ours. The blessings we've received come from a God who is the father of us all. Anytime we draw near to God, He will draw near to us. And that holds true for any and all of us.[58]

There is power in keeping our covenants. I have learned without equivocation that I can trust God in all areas of my life, that when I do what He asks He will sustain and support me. If I act with urgency on the spiritual promptings He gives me, it will always be at the right time: His time. There is a deep feeling of happiness and satisfaction that comes from making a difference in someone's life, and as we travel and teach these principles to others, we see the hope and light that fills their eyes as they too catch the same vision.

- Ginger L. Hitz, 2012

Notes

Endnotes

1 To discover your personal oil is to discover your life's calling, your passion, and your purpose. This idea was discussed in a speech given by James W. Ritchie, and alludes to a quote by J. Paul Getty: "Get up early, work hard, and find oil." See Ritchie, James W. "Find Your Oil; Make Your Mark." *Marriott Alumni Magazine*. Winter 2002: 16-17. Print.

2 "Search diligently, pray always, and be believing, and all things shall work together for your good, if ye walk uprightly and remember the covenant wherewith ye have covenanted one with another." Section 90: Verse 24. *The Doctrine and Covenants of The Church of Jesus Christ of Latter-Day Saints*. Salt Lake City: The Church of Jesus Christ of Latter-Day Saints, 1981. Print.

3 Jobs, Steve. "Commencement Address." Stanford University. Stanford, California. 12 June 2005. Keynote Address. Full speech printed in "'You've got to find what you love,' Jobs says." *Stanford Report* 14 June 2005. Print.

4 Ecclesiastes 3:1-4. *The Holy Bible*. King James Version. Print.

5 Oaks, Dallin H. "Timing." Brigham Young University. Provo, Utah. 29 January 2002. Published in *Brigham Young University 2001-2002: Speeches*. speeches.byu.edu. Web.

6 Page 190. Williamson, Marianne. *A Return to Love: Reflections on the Principles of A Course in Miracles*. New York: HarperPerennial, 1996. Print.

7 Mosiah 2:41. *The Book of Mormon: Another Testament of Jesus Christ*. Salt Lake City: The Church of Jesus Christ of Latter-Day Saints, 1981. Print.

₈ Galatians 6:8-9. *The Holy Bible*. King James Version. Print.

₉ See Benedict, Jeff. *How to Build a Business Warren Buffet Would Buy: The R.C. Willey Story*. Crawfordsville, Indiana: Shadow Mountain, 2009. Print.

₁₀ See Klinghoffer, David, and Joe Lieberman. *The Gift of Rest: Rediscovering the Beauty of the Sabbath*. New York: Howard Books, 2011. Print.

₁₁ 2 Kings 6:16. *The Holy Bible*. King James Version. Print.

₁₂ This teaching is repeated throughout the scriptures, a fact demonstrating the all-important nature of this philosophy. See Leviticus 19:18, Matthew 19:19, Matthew 22:39, Mark 12:31, Luke 10:27, Romans 13:9, Galatians 5:14, and James 2:8. *The Holy Bible*. King James Version. Print.

See also Section 59: Verse 6. *The Doctrine and Covenants of The Church of Jesus Christ of Latter-Day Saints*. Salt Lake City: The Church of Jesus Christ of Latter-Day Saints, 1981. Print.

₁₃ Refer to quote at beginning of this chapter: "No man can serve two masters: for either he will hate the one, and love the other; or else he will hold to the one, and despise the other. Ye cannot serve God and mammon." Matthew 6:24. *The Holy Bible*. King James Version. Print.

₁₄ "We have learned by sad experience that it is the nature and disposition of almost all men, as soon as they get a little authority, as they suppose, they will immediately begin to exercise unrighteous dominion." Section 121: Verse 39. *The Doctrine and Covenants of The Church of Jesus Christ of Latter-Day Saints*. Salt Lake City: The Church of Jesus Christ of Latter-Day Saints, 1981. Print.

15 Covey, Stephen M.R. *The Speed of Trust: The One Thing That Changes Everything*. New York: Free Press, 2006. Print.

16 Lencioni, Patrick. *The Five Dysfunctions of a Team: A Leadership Fable*. San Francisco: Jossey-Bass, 2002. Print.

17 Page 191. Ruff, Howard. *Safely Prosperous Or Really Rich: Choosing Your Personal Financial Heaven*. Hoboken, New Jersey: John Wiley & Sons, 2004. Print.

18 Smith, Hyrum W. "Speaking: Quotes from Hyrum." *HyrumWSmith*. Web.

19 Clason, George S. *The Richest Man in Babylon*. New York: Signet, 1988. Print.

20 See Covey, Stephen R. *The Seven Habits of Highly Effective People: Powerful Lessons in Personal Change*. New York: Free Press, 1989. Print.

See also Covey, Stephen M.R. *The Speed of Trust: The One Thing That Changes Everything*. New York: Free Press, 2006. Print.

21 Luke 22:41-42. *The Holy Bible*. King James Version.

22 Luke 22: 44. *The Holy Bible*. King James Version.

23 See Luke 10:37. *The Holy Bible*. King James Version.

24 Getty, J. Paul. *As I See It: The Autobiography of J. Paul Getty*. Englewood Cliffs, New Jersey: Prentice-Hall, 1976. Print.

25 "I, Nephi, having been born of goodly parents, therefore I was taught somewhat in all the learning of my father; and having seen

many afflictions in the course of my days, nevertheless, having been highly favored of the Lord in all my days; yea, having had a great knowledge of the goodness and the mysteries of God, therefore I make a record of my proceedings in my days." 1 Nephi 1:1. *The Book of Mormon: Another Testament of Jesus Christ.* Salt Lake City: The Church of Jesus Christ of Latter-Day Saints, 1981. Print.

26 Page 17. Dickens, Charles. *A Christmas Carol.* New York: Bantam Books, 1965. Print.

27 Pages 28-29. Gerber, Michael E. *The E-Myth Revisited: Why Most Small Businesses Don't Work and What to Do About It.* New York: HarperCollins, 1995. Print.

28 "…I perceive that thou art a sober child, and art quick to observe." Mormon 1:2. *The Book of Mormon: Another Testament of Jesus Christ.* Salt Lake City: The Church of Jesus Christ of Latter-Day Saints, 1981. Print.

29 Genesis 3:19. *The Holy Bible.* King James Version. Print.

30 Page 14. Clason, George S. *The Richest Man in Babylon.* New York: Signet, 1988. Print.

31 Page 14. Clason, George S. *The Richest Man in Babylon.* New York: Signet, 1988. Print.

32 The concept of the Personal Constitution was developed by Hyrum W. Smith and was an official product of both Franklin International Institute and Franklin Quest. Throughout this chapter, *The Ministry of Business* builds and expands upon Smith's original ideas.

33 Monson, Thomas S. "Finishers Wanted." *Ensign* June 1989. Print.

34 This pyramid is a modified version of the Franklin Covey Productivity Pyramid, the original of which may be viewed at the company's website (franklincovey.ro; or franklincovey.com).

35 Matthew 5:48. *The Holy Bible*. King James Version. Print.

36 I should note here that the only way to truly maximize these Productivity Points is to start your day early. I've never met anyone who I consider to be a real competitor who doesn't wake up around 5:30 every morning in order to "get after it" early.

37 Burg, Bob and John David Mann. *The Go-Giver: A Little Story About a Powerful Business Idea*. New York: Portfolio, 2007. Print.

38 Richard Ball is a successful entrepreneur and founding charter member of Launching Leaders. His words regarding the principle of giving back, as well as many other principles outlined in *The Ministry of Business* are included in the supplemental DVD, available at theministryofbusiness.com.

39 Mosiah 4:21. *The Book of Mormon: Another Testament of Jesus Christ*. Salt Lake City: The Church of Jesus Christ of Latter-Day Saints, 1981. Print.

40 Luke 6:38. *The Holy Bible*. King James Version. Print.

41 Mosiah 2:17. *The Book of Mormon: Another Testament of Jesus Christ*. Salt Lake City: The Church of Jesus Christ of Latter-Day Saints, 1981. Print.

42 Matthew 16:25-26. *The Holy Bible*. King James Version. Print.

43 "For dust thou art, and unto dust shalt thou return." Genesis 3:19. *The Holy Bible*. King James Version. Print.

[44] Rath, Tom. *Vital Friends: The People You Can't Afford to Live Without.* New York: Gallup Press, 2006. Print.

[45] Lencioni, Patrick. *Silos Politics and Turf Wars: A Leadership Fable About Destroying the Barriers That Turn Colleagues into Competitors.* San Francisco: Jossey-Bass, 2006. Print.

[46] Gerber, Michael E. *The E-Myth Revisited: Why Most Small Businesses Don't Work and What to Do About It.* New York: HarperCollins, 1995. Print.

[47] Little, Steven S. *The Milkshake Moment: Overcoming Stupid Systems, Pointless Policies, and Muddled Management to Realize Real Growth.* Hoboken, New Jersey: John Wiley & Sons, 2008. Print.

[48] Luke10:37. *The Holy Bible.* King James Version. Print.

[49] Kawasaki, Guy. *The Art of the Start: The Time-Tested, Battle-Hardened Guide for Anyone Starting Anything.* New York: Portfolio, 2004. Print.

[50] Benedict, Jeff. *How to Build a Business Warren Buffett Would Buy: The R.C. Willey Story.* Crawfordsville, Indiana: Shadow Mountain, 2009. Print.

[51] Kawasaki, Guy. *The Art of the Start: The Time-Tested, Battle-Hardened Guide for Anyone Starting Anything.* New York: Portfolio, 2004. Print.

[52] Covey, Stephen R. and Jennifer Colosimo. *Great Work, Great Career: How to Create Your Ultimate Job and Make an Extraordinary Contribution.* Salt Lake City, Utah: FranklinCovey, 2009. Print.

Collins, Jim. *Good to Great: Why Some Companies Make the Leap . . . and Others Don't.* New York: HarperCollins, 2001. Print.

[53] The concept of a Contribution Statement comes directly from *Great Work, Great Career: How to Create Your Ultimate Job and Make an Extraordinary Contribution* by Stephen R. Covey and Jennifer Colosimo.

[54] Monson, Thomas S. "In Quest of the Abundant Life." *Ensign* March 1988. Print.

[55] Quoted In: Page 127. Johnson, Lloyd Albert. *A Toolbox For Humanity: More Than 9000 Years of Thought, Volume 1: Responses to Nature and Ourselves*. Victoria, Canada: Trafford Publishing, 2003. Print.

[56] These interviews have been compiled into a supplementary DVD, available at theministryofbusiness.com.

[57] Jobs, Steve. "Commencement Address." Stanford University. Stanford, California. 12 June 2005. Keynote Address. Full speech printed in "'You've got to find what you love,' Jobs says." *Stanford Report* 14 June 2005. Print.

[58] "Draw nigh to God, and he will draw night to you. Cleanse your hands, ye sinners; and purify your hearts, ye double minded." *The Holy Bible*. King James Version. Print.

About The Authors

Steven A. Hitz—Steven A. Hitz, along with his wife, Ginger L. Hitz, founded US-Reports, Inc. in 1988. Since then, the company has grown to become the largest, uniquely structured corporate footprint of its kind, providing loss control, premium audit, and risk assessment services to over 500 insurance companies. In 2010, US-Reports became a member of The Kaufman Financial Group, the world's largest independent insurance broker. Steve still serves as CEO of the company.

Steve has long been passionate about working to achieve business innovation, and has surrounded himself with an astute team of gifted minds and hearts. In an effort to share this passion, he and Ginger are charter members of Launching Leaders, a career training and personal development program that has successfully graduated more than 200 students since its inception in 2011.

Along with their continued involvement with US-Reports, they continue operating other businesses involved with the banking, real estate, and farming industries. Steve and Ginger are the parents of three sons and two daughters, and they have five grandchildren.

 **James W. Ritchie**—Successful entrepreneur and executive James W. Ritchie has established himself as a prominent leader and teacher in the world of business. In 1969, he founded Ritchie Enterprises, LLC, before going on to create, lead, or advise a number of other profitable and successful business ventures. In 1989, Ritchie served as Senior Vice President for Franklin Quest (now FranklinCovey).

Since then, James and his wife, Carolyn Orton, have served in various councils and leadership positions at Brigham Young University, Brigham Young University–Hawaii, and Southern Virginia University. They have also served around the world in various volunteer capacities. James and Carolyn have eight children and 38 grandchildren.

Feel free to submit your comments or questions to:
theministryofbusiness@gmail.com